Whatever It Takes

PRAYING

Joe Engelkemier

HART RESEARCH CENTER
FALLBROOK, CALIFORNIA

Edited by Ken McFarland
Cover art direction and design by Ed Guthero
Cover illustration by Lars Justinen

The author assumes full responsibility for the
accuracy of all facts, quotations, and references as cited
in this book.

ISBN 1-878046-25-X

Contents

Introduction

"More than all we ask or imagine!"

Last week I had lunch with two Andrews University freshmen who had been reading the manuscript for this book. The suggestions they shared revealed a keen interest in prayer and a growing love for Jesus. One student said she had read Chapter 3—"Jesus Christ: Reason for Enthusiasm"—three times.

As we talked about making this book as helpful as possible to young people, another college freshman joined us and told us about her prayers for friends and classmates. She, too, was interested in learning more about prayer.

"Lord, teach us to pray," the disciples said to Jesus one morning (Luke 11:1). On another occasion they requested, "Lord, increase our faith," (Luke 17:5).

Are these your needs too? Would you, whatever your age, like to develop a better prayer life? Do you need a steadily growing confidence in God?

Prayer as a science

In the early 1970s I began teaching a "Workshop in Prayer" class at Andrews University. For it, I developed a study guide that I called the *Faith and Prayer* syllabus.

As I gathered content and illustrations, I discovered instruction about prayer in the writings of the prophets, in the Gospels, and all through the writings of Paul. Many of the Psalms are prayers. As for faith, the entire Bible seems designed to increase our trust in God.

I also discovered that the book *Education*, penned in 1903 by Ellen White, encourages a strong focus on faith and prayer *as a part of Christian education*. In a chapter entitled "Faith and Prayer," the author suggests that faith and prayer are closely allied and need to be studied together, adding:

> "In the prayer of faith there is a divine science; it is a science that everyone who would make his lifework a success must understand" (p. 257).

The implications are far-reaching. Even for *career* success, mothers and fathers need to teach their children about faith and prayer. Still another implication is that Christian high schools, colleges, and universities would do well to include courses about faith and about prayer in their curriculums. And might also the weeks of devotion conducted at Christian schools sometimes focus on developing a stronger faith and a richer prayer life?

The same author, in a chapter about the schools of the prophets, notes this:

> "A spirit of devotion was cherished. Not only were students taught the duty of prayer, but they were taught how to pray, how to approach their Creator, how to exercise faith in Him, and how to obey and understand the teachings of His Spirit" (*Patriarchs and Prophets*, p. 594).

In God's providence, the October, 1992, North American Division Year-end Meeting of Seventh-day Adventists developed two parallel themes: "Prayer Works!" and "Seeking His Spirit for Service."

Along with this volume, other materials supporting these twin themes include a book by Charles Bradford entitled *Find Out About Prayer,* a study guide by Kurt Johnson called *Prayer Works!* a video and study material by Ron Halverson entitled *Prayer Warriors,* a prayer journal by Dwight Nelson called *A New Way to Pray,* and a notebook by David and Gaylene Wolkwitz entitled *Holy Spirit Seminar.*

There is much excellent material on these subjects! In preparing this book and slanting it to youth, I am indebted to many authors. One book from which I received much help is S.D. Gordon's *Quiet Talks on Prayer*—a delightful book of sermons published nearly a hundred years ago!

Two recently published books that have enriched my own prayer life are Bob Beltz' *Transforming Your Prayer Life* and Bill Hybel's *Too Busy Not to Pray.* Other recent books to which I am indebted for ideas include Roger Dunn's *Don't Just Stand There—Pray Something,* and Leonard E. LeSourd's *Touching the Heart of God.*

Targeting youth

"Run," an angel was told in Zechariah's time, "speak to this young man" (Zechariah 2:4, KJV). In Bible times, those under 30 at the time of their call also included Esther, Samuel, Isaiah, Jeremiah, Ezekiel, Daniel, the mother of Jesus, possibly some of the twelve disciples, and Timothy. An Andrews University teacher, Bernard Lall, has written a book entitled *Prayer—Heaven's Unlimited Power at Our Disposal.* He includes a chapter he calls "Youth in Prayer." It's a beautiful sight, he suggests on page 111 of his book, to see young people kneeling together in prayer—praying for each other, praying for the church, praying for their parents, praying for revival.

The fall of 1970 brought just such a far-reaching revival to the campus of Andrews University. It started at a fall retreat. In the February, 1971 issue of *Ministry* magazine, E.L. Minchin wrote this about how it happened: "The topic of study at this retreat was prayer. The voluntary gathering of about ninety students, mostly undergraduate students, did just that—they prayed" (p. 6).

Lives were changed that weekend—and hundreds more during the weeks that followed. As the school year progressed, the influence spread to other denominational schools. Eventually, thousands of youth and others were drawn closer to Christ.

We again need the kind of renewal that occurred two decades ago at Andrews University. Secularism has lowered standards on many Christian campuses, and it is devastating thousands of Christian homes. Revival needs to take place all across North America. And throughout the entire world!

In his book *Master Preachers*, Harold C. Calkins reports that Charles Finney, who became president of Ohio's Oberlin College in 1851, sought "to have a revival among the students each year." This often happened, and one observer noted that "eighty-five per cent of the converts remained true to God" (p. 78).

Calkins reports that it was Bible study, prayer, and the Holy Spirit that brought revival (*Ibid.*, p. 79).

Whatever it takes

The early Christian Church gained life-changing power through prayer that was combined with a "whatever it takes" lifestyle. In Acts 1, the early church reached out to God in confession and prayer for ten days. Then in Acts 2, as Peter preached in the power of the Holy Spirit, 3,000 people made decisions for Christ. Within a single generation the message of Christ's love was taken to every part of the then-known world.

Today, as you build up your faith, as you pray, and as you reach out to others, God would love to use you in a similar way.

The "peaches and cream" part is this: through prayer, the study of God's Word, and ministry to others, we may enter into what one author calls the "closest intimacy" with God.

Millions have found that such intimacy and friendship bring almost unnumbered benefits—a stronger sense of God's presence, help with daily problems, forgiveness of sin, peace of mind, courage for daily living, and faith for the future.

Are you experiencing that intimate fellowship?

As you read this book, may these words of Paul describe your experience:

> "But you, dear friends, build yourselves up in
> your most holy faith and pray in the Holy Spirit.
> Keep yourselves in God's love as you wait for the
> grace of our Lord Jesus Christ to bring you to
> eternal life" (Jude 20, 21).

As you pray, and as you reach out in faith, you will discover something else: God "is able to do immeasurably more than all we ask or imagine, according to his power that is at work within us" (Ephesians 3:20)!

CHAPTER ONE

Whatever It Takes

The fall of the Berlin Wall in December of 1989 launched some of the swiftest changes our world has ever seen. The December 27, 1991 issue of *The Arizona Republic* cited an example from two days earlier:

> "On Dec. 25, the Soviet flag was lowered over the Kremlin, ending the brief existence of one of the most powerful, menacing but least successful empires history has known" (p. A-2).

The *Republic* noted that in August of 1991, "great chunks" of the empire began to fall away "with dizzying speed." The final hours, the paper added, were dreamlike in their swiftness.

Paul foresaw a time when God would intervene to "finish the work, and cut it short in righteousness" (Romans 9:28, KJV).

Has that time arrived?

As I write, tonight's paper carries this headline: "AIDS global forecast is grim." The opening paragraph of the article says:

"A new report on AIDS predicts a far grimmer future than previously forecast, warning that more than 100 million people on every corner of the Earth could be infected by the end of the decade" (*South Bend Tribune*, June 4, 1992, p. 1).

If that does happen, how long will it take for 100 million to become 200 million? And if a cure isn't found, how long will it take for 200 million to become 400 million?

Has the time come for some changes in our priorities?

Giving priority to prayer

"Prayer," H.M.S. Richards, Sr. observed, "is the most talked about and least practiced of all Christian beliefs."

Everyone loses when we neglect to pray. The family loses when regular times for worship and secret prayer get crowded out. The church weakens when its members neglect Bible study, mediation, and prayer. The cause of Christ dips in spirituality when not much praying is going on.

God told Abraham, "I will bless you . . . and you will be a blessing" (Genesis 12:2). That promise is also for every believer today. Key ways in which God's children can be a blessing to others include:

1. Through what they are.
2. Through what they say.
3. Through their service.
4. Through money invested in the work of God.
5. Through their prayers.[1]

Probably most would agree that the first—the character of an individual—largely determines the value of the other four. But after that, which of the other four do you see as having potential for the most far-reaching influence?

Could it be that the ministry with the most potential for good is our prayers?

Here's why. The touch of a godly life is usually local. The power for good through use of the lips is usually quite limited also. And even large sums of money can do only so much. But prayer can go anywhere, at any time of the day or night. Through prayer we can spend time in—and bring blessings to—any region or city or nation on earth. And our prayers give Jesus Christ—our "Mighty Conqueror"—an undisputed right to act.

A revival of Bible study, too

During another troubled era, Jeremiah wrote, "Thy words were found, and I ate them; and thy words became to me a joy and the delight of my heart" (Jeremiah 15:16, RSV). *A joy! The delight of my heart!*

Could a revival of Jeremiah's kind of Bible study bring hope to the discouraged? Would it increase our power in prayer? Would it produce a greater trust in God?

On a South Pacific battlefield during World War II, Randy staggered and pitched forward. A searing pain surged through his body. Sudden darkness made it impossible to see. Then, as companions attempted to get him to a first-aid

---

A revival of Bible study is needed throughout the world. As this takes place, lives will be transformed, and a knowledge of God will cover the earth as the waters cover the sea.

---

station, an exploding bomb hit even closer. More terrible wounds. More pain.

Randy eventually ended up in a hospital in Australia. He had lost his sight, both arms, and both legs.

Randy asked a nurse to write a letter for him to a pastor. This is what he had her write:

"Sir, ten years ago I gave my heart to God. They have been the happiest years of my life. Now I have no legs and I have no arms and I have no eyes, but praise God I have a nose. Would you please find a Bible for me written in Braille, so that I can learn to read it with my nose?"

Randy got the Bible he requested. A nurse propped it up before him, and he learned to read with his nose. He made no complaints. "He is an inspiration to everyone," one nurse commented.[2]

A revival of Bible study is needed throughout the world. Such a revival will transform thousands of lives. A knowledge of God will cover the earth the way the waters cover the sea.

What would it take to bring about a worldwide revival of Bible study? What would it take for us to develop unlimited trust in God?

"Whatever it takes"

A Midwest auto agency recently offered to do "whatever it takes" to get customers into one of their new cars. Not long after I heard that commercial, I read about an eleven-year-old South Bend, Indiana, boy named Jason Strahla, who had been born with a cleft lip and a disfigured face. His trips to a plastic surgeon began when he was six days old. He had undergone forty-seven surgeries, with still more to come.

The South Bend *Tribune* article about Jason told of his determination. "He's somebody that will not give up," said Larry Sargent, his surgeon. "He's willing to do what it takes to get better."[3]

Throughout history individuals and groups have been willing to do "whatever it takes" to achieve a desired purpose. In the Bible Paul illustrates that spirit. One time he listed some of the things he had experienced—five whippings, two beatings with rods, three shipwrecks, long journeys, dangers, hunger, thirst, cold, and nakedness (2 Cor. 11:24-28). That's quite a "whatever it takes"[4] list! With that spirit Paul and the other early believers took the gospel to the then-known world in a single generation.

Another example

"Tell that man he is forgiven," a pastor said as he lay dying of stab wounds. The pastor had started a mission in a Hindu-dominated part of India. One day a leader came to see him and requested prayer. Hoping to lead his visitor to Christ, the pastor took him to a side room. As he prayed, the visitor pulled out a knife and stabbed him repeatedly.

Three days later, knowing that his end was near, the pastor made the above request of his son. He then added: "Care for your mother and carry on this ministry. Do whatever it takes to win people to Christ."[5]

Whatever it takes! Some 6,000 years earlier, at "a council of peace" (Zechariah 6:13, KJV), the three Executives who run this universe made a similar decision. They would do "whatever it takes" to save a fallen planet. And they would do so even though this world is only a tiny speck in a universe of hundreds of billions of galaxies!

Whatever it takes! In Philippians 2:6-9 Paul tells what it did take: Jesus Christ, One equal with God—and Co-creator and Co-ruler of all these galaxies—"humbled himself and became obedient to death—even death on a cross" (v. 8).

A "Whatever it takes" parable

Wherever He went Jesus attracted tax collectors, prostitutes, and other outcasts. One day when His audience included some of these people, Pharisees stood at the edge of the crowd and grumbled, "This man welcomes sinners and eats with them" (Luke 15:2).

Jesus decided to let His critics know that even social outcasts matter to God. Instead of one story, He told three. Here's the first:

> "Suppose one of you has a hundred sheep and loses one of them. Does he not leave the ninety-nine in the open country and go after the lost sheep until he finds it? And when he finds it, he joyfully puts it on his shoulders and goes home. Then he calls his friends and neighbors together and says, 'Rejoice with me; I have found my lost sheep.' I tell you that in the same way there will be more rejoicing in heaven over one sinner who

repents than over ninety-nine righteous persons
who do not need to repent" (Luke 15:4-7).

Three truths leap out at us:
1. Lost sheep matter to a shepherd.
In the parable, only one out of a hundred was lost.
That's a mere one percent! But that one percent mattered!
**2. No matter what the risk, a caring shepherd goes
after lost sheep.**
The author of *Christ's Object Lessons* suggests that the
search of Luke 15 took place on a stormy night. The
shepherd "climbs the steepest heights, he goes to the very
edge of the precipice, at the risk of his own life" (p. 188).
As he hears a faint cry down on a cliff, he presses toward
the lost lamb. He will do whatever it takes to rescue it.
3. Finding the lost awakens gratitude and joy.
In the parable, the lost sheep does not get scolded. It
does not get driven with a whip. The shepherd doesn't even
try to lead it. He picks up the trembling creature. If it is
bruised, he presses it to his bosom so that the warmth of
his own heart may give it life. As he carries it back to the
fold, he does so with gratitude and joy.

All three Luke 15 parables picture concern for the lost.
The first two—the lost sheep and the lost coin—focus on
the "whatever it takes" effort expended. All three end with
rejoicing. In the third—that of the lost son—one senses
that the father had done a lot of praying.

Is there a parallel for today? Shouldn't we be seeking
the lost with a "whatever it takes" spirit? And shouldn't
that seeking be backed with "whatever it takes" praying?

Unprecedented results

As I think and pray about our need to reach lost people,
my thoughts keep going to Isaiah 60 through 62. Chapter
60 begins with this appeal to the church:

> "Arise, shine, for your light has come, and the
> glory of the Lord rises upon you. See, darkness
> covers the earth and thick darkness is over the

peoples, but the Lord rises upon you and his glory appears over you. Nations will come to your light, and kings to the brightness of your dawn" (Isaiah 60:1-3).

The first part of chapter 61 is a Messianic prophecy. It describes the methods Christ used to win hurting and lost people. He preached good news, bound up the brokenhearted, proclaimed freedom to captives, banished darkness, comforted those who mourned, and gave beauty in place of ashes (vv. 1-3).

We, too, need to use those methods. The balance of Isaiah 61 describes what the results will be when we do so. Thousands and even millions will find salvation, exclaiming:

"I delight greatly in the Lord, my soul rejoices in my God. For he has clothed me with garments of salvation and arrayed me in a robe of righteousness, as a bridegroom adorns his head like a priest, and as a bride adorns herself with her jewels" (Isaiah 61:10). "For as the soil makes the sprout come up and a garden causes seeds to grow," chapter 61 concludes, "so the Sovereign Lord will make righteousness and praise spring up before all nations" (Isaiah 61:12).

Isaiah 62 includes a call to prayer—an invitation to give God "no rest" until He makes Jerusalem the "praise of the earth" (vv. 6, 7). Through their unbelief the Hebrew people lost that privilege. It now belongs to the believers of today.

The most fruitful soil

Much of earth's final harvest probably will come from people in their teens or early twenties. According to Faith for Today Speaker-Director Dan Matthews, "After the age of 25, only one in 10,000 will ever become a Christian."[6]

In Europe and North America almost one-fourth of the population is under 15. And with a few exceptions such as Japan, 40 to 45 percent of the people in the non-western world are under 15.[7]

That means that by A.D. 2000, when the expected world population will pass 6 billion, at least 2 billion will be people under 15! That's more than 140 million 14-year-olds! And another 140 million 13-year-olds! And a similar number for each age level down to birth!

Could I say something just to those of you who are in high school or college? Could it be that you are the ones most able to reach other youth? As God leads, are you willing to reach out to at least one person close to your age?

What might happen if each Christian young person would ask God to lead him or her to a non-believing acquaintance about the same age?

What if each then built a redemptive—but not romantic—friendship with that person? Could tens of thousands be brought to Christ?

> "Christ's method alone will give true success in reaching the people. The Saviour mingled with men as one who desired their highest good. He showed His sympathy for them, ministered to their needs, and won their confidence. Then He bade them 'Follow me'" (*The Ministry of Healing*, p. 143).

Notice the steps in this "strategy for success": (1) mingling with people, (2) showing sympathy for them, (3) ministering to their needs, (4) winning their confidence, and (5) inviting a decision.

Whatever You want/Whatever it takes

As a summary of His lifestyle, Christ spoke of His Father, and said: "I always do what pleases Him" (John 8:29). Combine that "Whatever You want" with "Whatever it takes"! The result makes for a life of almost unlimited potential for good!

The author of *The Desire of Ages* suggests that he who loves Jesus the most will do the most good, and adds, "There is no limit to the usefulness of one who, by putting self aside, makes room for the working of the Holy Spirit upon his heart, and lives a life wholly consecrated to God" (pp. 250, 251).

Is that what you want? Would you be interested in developing a "whatever it takes" spirit in your prayer life? Would you like to pray with a stronger confidence in God? And are you willing to back your prayers with a "whatever You want" and "whatever it takes" lifestyle?

Through Christ, there could stretch before you a future of unlimited usefulness! And an eternity filled with the joy and splendor of having turned "many to righteousness" (Daniel 12:3)!

Notes

1. Adapted from S.D. Gordon, *Quiet Talks on Prayer* (New York: Grosset & Dunlap, 1904), pp. 10, 11.

2. E.L. Minchin, "The Great Secret," *Review and Herald*, Sept. 2, 1954, p. 10.

3. Joseph Dits, "Boy Comes Face to Face With Hope," *South Bend Tribune*, September, 1992.

4. In this book, the expression "whatever it takes"— sometimes "WIT"—means "whatever it takes within Scriptural boundaries." That usage precludes any violation of integrity. It also precludes neglect of family responsibilities or engaging in excessive labor.

5. Bill Hybels, *Too Busy Not to Pray*, (Downers Grove, Illinois: Intervarsity Press, 1988), p. 63. Used by permission.

6. Dan Matthews, *Faith For Today Report*, February, 1982, p. 11.

7. *Population and Development Review* (New York: The Population Council, Inc., June, 1983), p. 331.

CHAPTER TWO

We Need Nehemiahs!

C an "whatever it takes" praying, combined with "whatever it takes" living, accomplish the apparently impossible?

The book of Nehemiah relates an example: Through Nehemiah's prayers and influence, an unfinished task that had lingered for more than sixty years was completed *in just fifty-two days!*

About 450 B.C., the people in Jerusalem probably thought that they would never again enjoy security. Some sixty years earlier, the returned exiles had rebuilt the temple. The walls of Jerusalem had also been partly reconstructed. But after that, nothing much had been done.

Then around 450 B.C., enemies destroyed most of the rebuilt sections. If you had lived then, you would have had every reason to be frightened. Wild beasts roamed the woods and fields. Bands of robbers wandered through the countryside to plunder and kill. The wall about a town or city often meant the difference between a night of peaceful sleep and a night filled with fear.

To the residents of Jerusalem, it must have seemed they would always be living in fear.

Nehemiah learned about these new dangers while serving at the palace of King Artaxerxes at Susa. About December of the twentieth year of Artaxerxes' reign, Nehemiah's brother Hanani and other visitors from Judah came to the Persian capital.

> "'Those who survived the exile and are back in the province are in great trouble and disgrace,' they told Nehemiah. 'The wall of Jerusalem is broken down, and its gates have been burned with fire'" (Nehemiah 1:3).

When he heard this, Nehemiah sat down and wept. "For some days," he said, "I mourned and fasted and prayed before the God of heaven" (Nehemiah 1:4).

The next seven verses record his prayer—a petition that provides a good pattern when you need to ask God to do something. Notice these four parts:

1. Adoration. He addresses his Creator as a "great and awesome God" (v. 5).

2. Confession. Nehemiah confesses his sins and the sins of his people (vv. 6, 7).

3. Confidence. He cites promises from the book of Deuteronomy with confidence that they will be fulfilled (vv. 8-10).

4. Commitment. He is willing for God to use him to help bring an answer to his own prayer (v. 11).

A plan

While Nehemiah prayed, a plan came to his mind. As cupbearer for Artaxerxes, he would speak to the king about the situation in Jerusalem. He ended his prayer with this plea: "O Lord, let your ear be attentive to the prayer of this your servant. . . . Give your servant success today by granting him favor in the presence of this man" (Nehemiah 1:11).

An opportunity did not come that day, however. Nor the next. Nor the next. But Nehemiah kept praying.

As he prayed, his faith and courage increased. The

author of *Prophets and Kings* summarizes the spirit of his prayers:

> "His mouth was filled with holy arguments. He pointed to the dishonor that would be cast upon God, if His people, now that they had returned to Him, should be left in weakness and oppression" (p. 629).

Nehemiah backed his "arguments" with Scripture cited from Deuteronomy 4:29-31. God had warned that sin could cause His people to be scattered to the ends of the earth. But He also promised that upon repentance, He would restore them to their homes. Nehemiah was confident the Lord would fulfill that promise.

Nehemiah's "arguing with God" and his claiming of promises continued for four months. And the longer he prayed, the stronger his concern became.

That concern eventually helped open a door of opportunity. Nehemiah spent so much time in confession of sin and in earnest pleading that it began to tell on his health.

One day in the spring, as he took the king's wine to him, Artaxerxes eyed him suspiciously. "Why does your face look so sad when you are not ill?" the king asked. "This can be nothing but sadness of heart" (Nehemiah 2:2).

That frightened Nehemiah. He feared that Artaxerxes would think he was part of a plot to overthrow him. Nehemiah explained the cause for his concern, and the king asked, "What is it that you want?"

Before he replied, Nehemiah darted a silent prayer to heaven. "I prayed to the God of heaven," he said (Nehemiah 2:4). That quick prayer won to his side a power that could turn the heart of even a heathen king. And Nehemiah didn't just ask for permission to go. He also requested a safe-conduct and supplies.

"Because the gracious hand of my God was upon me," Nehemiah reported, "the king granted my request" (Nehemiah 2:8).

More prayer

When Nehemiah arrived in Jerusalem, he found a discouraged people. The third night there, he took a few trusted men and surveyed the broken-down walls and the burned gates.

> "The officials did not know where I had gone or what I was doing," he later wrote, "because as yet I had said nothing to the Jews or the priests or nobles or officials" (Nehemiah 2:16).

He spent the rest of the night in prayer. He knew that he would need the power of God the next morning as he tried to rouse his dispirited countrymen.

God spoke through him. "Come, let us rebuild the wall of Jerusalem," he urged (Nehemiah 2:17). He reinforced his request with a faith-building testimony: "I also told them about the gracious hand of my God upon me and what the king had said to me" (Nehemiah 2:18).

That brought a positive response! "Let us start rebuilding," the people said (Nehemiah 2:18).

With a "whatever it takes" spirit, Nehemiah threw everything he had into the work. This summarizes his influence:

> "His holy purpose, his high hope, his cheerful consecration to the work, were contagious. The people caught the enthusiasm of their leader, and in his sphere each man became a Nehemiah" (Ellen White, *SDA Bible Commentary*, vol. 3, p. 1137).

Nehemiah kept in close touch with the workers. He spoke courage to the fearful and words of approval to the diligent. He prayed fervently and constantly. "The God of heaven," he exclaimed again and again, "He will give us success" (Nehemiah 2:20).

More "whatever it takes"

The WIT spirit of the builders continues strong in Nehemiah 4. The chapter begins by telling about the mockery and ridicule of Sanballat and certain enemies (vv. 1-3). Nehemiah responded by going to his knees in prayer (vv. 4, 5). In the next verse, he gave this report: "So we rebuilt the wall till all of it reached half its height, for the people worked with all their heart" (v. 6).

But then Sanballat and his allies developed plans to attack the workers. This was a call to more prayer, of which Nehemiah wrote, "We prayed to our God and posted a guard day and night to meet this threat" (v. 9).

Then another problem arose: certain workers from the tribe of Judah got discouraged and complained, "The strength of the laborers is giving out, and there is so much rubble that we cannot rebuild the wall" (v. 10).

To make things still more difficult, some Jews who lived close to the Sanballat camp became frightened. They came to Nehemiah with warnings that the workers would be killed. And they didn't come just once. "The Jews who lived near them," Nehemiah reported, "came and told us ten times over, 'Wherever you turn, they will attack you'" (v. 12).

Ten times over! That could get discouraging!

But Nehemiah's "whatever it takes" spirit remained strong. He stationed guards at the most exposed places. "Don't be afraid," he told the people. Then, in words reminiscent of the adoration in his chapter 1 prayer, he added: "Remember the Lord, who is great and awesome, and fight for your brothers, your sons and daughters, your wives and your homes" (v. 14).

Nehemiah divided his men into two groups. "Half my men did the work, while the other half were equipped with spears, shields, bows and armor," he wrote (v. 16). Those who carried materials did so with one hand; they carried a weapon in the other. Each builder wore his sword at his side as he worked.

These closing verses of chapter 4 reflect the spirit of the entire chapter:

> "So we continued the work with half the men holding spears, from the first light of dawn till the stars came out. At that time I also said to the people, 'Have every man and his helper stay inside Jerusalem at night, so they can serve us as guards by night and workmen by day.' Neither I nor my brothers nor my men nor the guards with me took off our clothes; each had his weapon, even when he went for water" (vv. 21-23).

More problems arose in chapter 5, and still more in the first part of chapter 6. But near the end of chapter 6, Nehemiah gives this report: "So the wall was completed on the twenty-fifth of Elul [August-September], in fifty-two days" (v. 15).

Fifty-two days!

"We need Nehemiahs"

Do you see a parallel for the 1990s?

Revelation 14 introduces an angel flying through the heavens with what John called "the eternal gospel"—a gospel to be taken "to every nation, tribe, language, and people" (Revelation 14:6).

This angel is followed by two more—each with a distinctive end-time message. All are obviously symbolic, for the work assigned to them is that of preaching the everlasting gospel. That preaching has not been entrusted to literal angels; it has been committed to men. Each of these angels, therefore, symbolizes those who are commissioned to make known to the world the gospel *and* the special truths which constitute the burden of each angel's message.

Revelation 14:12 describes the kind of people the messages of Revelation 14:6-11 produce: "Here is the patience of the saints: here are they that keep the commandments of God, and the faith of Jesus." The last seven verses of Revelation 14 then describe the second coming of Jesus. This indicates that these messages are to be given to the world *just before Christ returns*. And they are to go to every nation, to every island, to every people group.

In a world were the population increases by more than seventy million people every twelve months, that's a task far more challenging than rebuilding some stone walls!

But with God nothing is impossible. God is well able "to do immeasurably more than all we ask or imagine" (Ephesians 3:20).

Why, then, are there hundreds of millions who have never heard the name of Jesus? And why are there still vast multitudes of people who know nothing of the special truths of Revelation 14?

The Laodician message of Revelation 3 pinpoints a key reason: lukewarmness. "I know your deeds," says the True Witness, "that you are neither cold nor hot" (v. 15).

What's the solution?

We need Nehemiahs!

At the start of the Jerusalem project, there was only one Nehemiah. But one became several. Several became dozens. Dozens became hundreds and possibly thousands.

Could that be the challenge for the rest of this decade?

Whatever your position—a young person still in school, lay person, church officer, pastor, church administrator, worker in supporting ministries—could you exert a Nehemiah-like influence as we continue through the 1990s?

Qualities that make a difference

Note again these words about Nehemiah: *"His holy purpose, his high hope, his cheerful consecration to the work, were contagious. The people caught the enthusiasm of their leader, and in his sphere each man became a Nehemiah."*

A similar description in *Prophets and Kings* also mentions Nehemiah's energy and determination (p. 638).

Consider the qualities that gave Nehemiah such a positive influence:

A holy purpose. Nehemiah sought nothing for himself. He wanted only to bring glory to God and security to his people.

A high hope. He didn't dwell on the sins of the people or scold them for their lukewarmness. He compiled no list of quotations about the shortcomings of the people. With an optimistic spirit, he spoke words of faith and hope—and backed those words with a testimony of what God had done for him.

A cheerful consecration. He wasn't just committed; he was *cheerfully* committed. And cheerfulness, like enthusiasm, is contagious.

Energy. *Energy* is defined as vitality of expression, a capacity for acting, a capacity for work. Nehemiah had developed each of these characteristics.

Determination.   No hindrance, no threat, no discouragement kept Nehemiah from pressing ahead.

The power of godly enthusiasm

Enthusiasm about a lot of things—a sports victory, a human achievement, a popular leader—tends to be short-lived. Professional tennis player Chris Evert, who played 1,144 matches during her career, once said that the thrill of victory "lasts about an hour" (*Newsweek*, July 17, 1989, p. 47).

The word *enthusiasm* comes from *en theos*, the Greek for *in God*. That's the kind of enthusiasm that lasts—enthusiasm for the things of God.

We need men, women, youth and children who are seeking to develop and strengthen the qualities of Nehemiah. *We need Nehemiahs!*

Let each of us also learn to pray with Nehemiah's "whatever it takes" spirit. Miracles of grace would then begin to take place! The visions of the prophets about a witness that reaches every nation and language and people would then be fulfilled!

Early Christians quickly took the gospel to all the then-known world (Colossians 1:23).

"The commission that Christ gave to the disciples, they fulfilled. As these messengers went forth to proclaim the gospel, there was such a revelation of the glory of God as had never before been witnessed by mortal man. By the co-operation of the divine Spirit, the apostles did a work that shook the world. To every nation was the gospel carried in a single generation" (*Acts of the Apostles*, p. 593).

Could something similar happen again? How about during this decade?

Fully committed disciples

"The eyes of the Lord," a prophet once said, "range throughout the earth to strengthen those whose hearts are fully committed to him" (2 Chronicles 16:9).

Fully committed disciples!

Another term being used today is *radical discipleship*. A disciple is someone who accepts and helps spread the doctrines of another. A radical, fully committed disciple of Jesus totally accepts and earnestly seeks to share His teachings—doing it with a *whatever You say* and a *whatever it takes* commitment.

Radical discipleship finds its strength in Bible study and prayer. Along with a whatever it takes spirit, such a disciple cherishes a strong sense of dependance upon Jesus.

"Apart from me," Jesus said, "you can do nothing" (John 15:5). He went on to explain the secret for getting answers to prayer and for becoming a fruit-bearing disciple:

"If you remain in me and my words remain in you, ask whatever you wish, and it will be given you. This is to my Father's glory, that you bear much fruit, showing yourselves to be my disciples" (John 15:7, 8).

In the weeks and months ahead, it is my desire and purpose to:

■ Seek an ever-increasing confidence in the God who did so much for and through Nehemiah.

■ Cultivate the character qualities that Nehemiah possessed.

■ Always be optimistic about the power of the eternal gospel to change lives.

■ Develop an increased conviction that every person within my sphere of influence matters to God—and should therefore matter to me.

■ Pray with a "whatever it takes" spirit—submitting to God with a "whatever You want" spirit and with a commitment to do whatever I can to help bring about the desired results.

With Christ's help, will you join me in seeking to become a Nehemiah? Will you join me in a determination to become a radical and fully committed disciple of Jesus Christ?

CHAPTER THREE

Jesus Christ: Reason for Enthusiasm

C an an enthusiasm such as Nehemiah's last over the long haul? Put Nehemiah into the 1990s. Make him a part of your local church—a youth leader, the head elder, the personal ministries director, the pastor, whoever. Would his enthusiasm last? Would it be contagious?

The experts claim that enthusiasm *can* be maintained. But only *if* an individual really believes in someone or something. New Testament Christianity offers both. Jesus Christ is the *Someone*. What He offers is the *something*.

This chapter directs attention to Jesus as a Person—His character, His personality, what people like about Him. In the next chapter we will survey what Christianity offers.

Friendship opportunities

What chance do you have of becoming a good friend of some really important person? How about a close friendship with a top executive in a major corporation, for example? Or with a sports hero you admire? Or with the President of the United States?

Better still, how would you like to develop friendships with several such people?

For most of us, there's zero chance for any of the above. But consider something that *is* an option: daily fellowship with the three Executives who run the universe.

Most people probably don't think of it that way, but isn't that exactly what genuine prayer offers?

On the evening before His crucifixion, Jesus talked about friendship. And He spoke about it in relationship to Himself, His Father, and the Holy Spirit.

That talk is recorded in John 14-16. Jesus included us when He said, "I have loved you" (John 15:12). Then He added, "Greater love has no one than this, that he lay down his life for his friends" (John 15:13).

"You are my friends," He continued, "if you do what I command. I no longer call you servants. . . . Instead, I have called you friends, for everything that I learned from my Father I have made known to you" (John 14:14, 15).

Incredible! Three times in four verses Christ calls us friends! The Co-Creator of the entire universe comes to us and offers to become our special Friend!

Are you finding maximum enjoyment in that friendship?

Prayer has been called "opening the heart to God as to a friend." Thus, the better we understand what God is like, the more we will enjoy talking to Him and listening to Him.

But what is God really like? For a picture of Him, we look at Jesus. Every admirable quality in Christ is also found in the Father. The resemblance is so close that Jesus once told His disciples, "He who has seen me has seen the Father" (John 14:9).

The same can be said about the Holy Spirit. The Holy Spirit, in fact, is sometimes called "the Spirit of Christ" (Romans 8:9; 1 Peter 1:11). Every personality attraction found in Jesus is also found in the Holy Spirit.

Let me attempt the impossible: painting a word picture of what Jesus is like. I'll start with a brief glimpse of His youth.

Seventeen and Rugged

Imagine yourself as seventeen. If you aren't there yet, fast forward to your seventeenth birthday. If you are beyond that, try to recall the day your turned seventeen.

Then go back to the time when Jesus was growing up in Nazareth. Picture Him as seventeen, like yourself. What kind of seventeen-year-old would He have been? Would you and He have been good friends?

The gospels don't say much about Christ's childhood and youth. Mark and John tell nothing. Matthew mentions Mary's pregnancy, the wise men, the flight to Egypt, and the return to Nazareth. But he says nothing about Christ's childhood years or His youth.

Luke gives a couple of hints. Before he tells about Christ's visit to Jerusalem as a twelve-year-old, Luke says this about His childhood: "And the child grew and became strong in spirit, filled with wisdom, and the grace of God was upon him" (Luke 2:40).

A similar statement is made about His cousin John: "The child grew and became strong in spirit, and lived in the desert until he appeared to Israel" (Luke 1:80).

The expression "strong in spirit" says something about the childhood and youth of both Christ and John. Neither succumbed to peer pressure. Had you been a seventeen-year-old neighbor of Christ, you could have been very comfortable in His presence. His strength would have strengthened you.

You would have found the seventeen-year-old Jesus to be physically rugged. He put in long hours in a carpenter shop—and carpenter work in His day developed muscles. His mother would have taught Him what Proverbs says about diligence. You would have found Him consistently modeling that trait. The furniture that He made in the carpenter shop would have been as perfect as human skill can produce.

You would have found that He regarded His body to be a temple for the Holy Spirit. Physically as well as spiritually, He lived in harmony with God's laws. His example would have helped motivate you to keep your body healthy and strong.

Fun to be with

I believe you would have enjoyed—immensely enjoyed—time with Jesus as a seventeen-year-old. The same verse that says He was "strong in spirit" also describes Him as "filled with wisdom." Then it says that "the grace of God was upon Him" (Luke 2:40).

Those qualities add excellence to friendship! You would have learned much from visiting with Him. He was already developing ideas that He would share more than a decade later in His ministry. And best of all, in associating with Him, you would be adding to your own wisdom and grace. But that's not all! The "by-beholding-we-become-changed" law would have worked powerfully in your life.

As His neighbor, you could have watched with Him as a storm moved inland from the Mediterranean, as described in Psalm 27. As thunder roared, you could have talked together about God's power. If a rainbow appeared as the storm moved out toward the desert, your youthful Companion might have said something about the hope and mercy the rainbow represented.

Christ loved the out-of-doors. On springtime Sabbath afternoons, you could have hiked together through the hills to identify wildflowers or do bird watching. By rising early in winter, you could have seen Orion in the Palestine sky. You could have knelt together to pray as the dawn began to lighten the east.

Christ's "full-of-wonder" personality

Christ began His ministry at thirty years of age. Let's imagine that you—now in your thirties—still live in

Nazareth. How would you describe the character and personality of your Friend?

Webster defines character as a person's mental and ethical traits—qualities such as honesty, for example. Personality is the total person—one's character, attitudes, and habits.

Cruden's Concordance lists nearly 140 different names and titles for Christ—ranging from Advocate to Worthy. Each tells or implies something about His personality and character.

The title of **Captain** (Hebrews 2:10) suggests competence and leadership skills. **King of kings** (Revelation 19:10) indicates dignity, authority, kingliness. **Servant** (Isaiah 42:1) points to qualities such as humility, willingness to serve, and devotion. **Living water** (John 4:10, 14) implies Someone refreshing in personality and temperament. It reminds us, also, of His ability to cleanse and to purify.

Creator (Isaiah 43:15) directs attention to His power and creativity. Think, for example, of the variety He used in making plants and animals. I've read that there are 300 varieties of sweet peas! Probably thousands of varieties of trees—and of wildflowers, of grasses, and of birds. Even with snowflakes, supposedly no two are exactly alike.

As the **Morning Star** (Revelation 22:16), Christ exemplifies characteristics such as hopefulness, encouragement, optimism. As the **Sun of Righteousness** (Malachi 4:2), He brings life and growth.

Glance back over these names. Imagine a friend with the qualities these names represent, as listed here:

- Competent

- Skilled in leadership

- Dignified

- Possessing authority

- Kingly

- Humble

- Willing to serve

- Refreshing
- Able to cleanse
- Invigorating
- Creative
- Imaginative
- Hopeful
- Encouraging
- Optimistic
- Life-giving
- Growth-producing
- Sunny in disposition

What kind of list might you put together if you examined *all* of Christ's 140 titles?

Very human—yet more than human

Jesus had a favorite title for Himself—"the Son of Man." He used it nearly sixty times in the gospels.

I love that fact about Christ! As a man, He wants to be a trusted Companion to every man. He seeks to impart courage—and beauty—to every woman. He desires the devotion of every teenager. He seeks the love of every child.

He was and is more than just a Man, however. The Bible presents Him as the co-Creator of all the hundreds of billions of galaxies in known space. John wrote, "Through Him all things were made; without him nothing was made that has been made" (John 1:3).

"His goings out," wrote Micah, had been "from the days of eternity" (5:2, KJV). He knows the name of each star and galaxy—He "brings out the starry host" and "calls them each by name" (Isaiah 40:6).

Before becoming a man, He had traveled "from star to star, from world to world, superintending all, by His providence supplying the needs of every order of being in His vast creation" (*Patriarchs and Prophets*, p. 69).

And a "vast creation" it is!

His galactic empire

"Lift your eyes and look at the heavens," God invites (Isaiah 40:26). With the naked eye, we see about 3,000 stars in each hemisphere. Most are comparatively close neighbors.

We also see the merged light of billions of stars within the Milky Way. The stars—suns—in this "river of light" appear to touch each other, but a telescope reveals that vast distances separate them. The average distance between stars is about six light-years.

(A light-year is the distance that light travels in a year—at eleven million miles a minute, sixteen billion miles every twenty-four hours, six trillion miles every year!)

Our Galaxy contains at least 100 billion sun. Few can grasp how much one billion is. For example:

■ There have been only a little over one billion minutes since the birth of Christ.

■ If you had inherited a billion dollars at the time of Christ and had spent $1,000 a day ever since, you would still have enough money left to keep on spending $1,000 a day for another 750 years!

The billions of suns in our Galaxy are arranged in the shape of a huge spiral similar to the diagram on the right. Our sun is located about three-fifths of the way out from the center. When we look out from the plane of this disk-like spiral, we see individual stars. When we look toward the center of the spiral, as we do in the summer in this hemisphere, we get a milky effect from the merged light of millions of suns.

God's greatness and splendor

Most astronomy books suggest that our Galaxy is about 100,000 light-years across and about 2,000 light years

Imagine crossing it from rim to rim in a Boeing 747! At 600 miles an hour, it would take 115 billion years to cross![1]

There are hundreds of billions of galaxies within known space. The next time you look at the Big Dipper, consider this: if you could see the bowl of that Dipper the way a large telescope views and photographs it, you would find a million galaxies just in the bowl![2]

David wrote, "The heavens declare the glory of God" (Psalm 19:1). As telescopes probe deeper and deeper into space, we can only exclaim, "Yours, O Lord, is the greatness and the power and the glory and the majesty and the splendor!" (1 Chronicles 29:11).

Loved by children

Solomon spoke of "the heaven of heavens" (1 Kings 8:27, KJV)—a place that probably is the administrative center of this huge universe. Try to picture Christ in His pre-incarnation splendor. In your imagination, see Him as He helps His Father administer the affairs of their immense creation.

Stand with Christ in that "heaven of heavens" and look out into space. See the galaxies and the clusters of galaxies!

Then see Christ on this planet as "the Son of Man." Watch as He cleanses the temple on the Sunday afternoon before His crucifixion. See the terrified money-changers and Pharisees as they drive their cattle before them.

As you stand there, you notice the people who didn't

You watch as an Intergalactic Executive from the administrative center of the universe tenderly holds two children on His lap.

---

flee—the lame, the blind, the deaf, and many children. They crowd about Jesus. He heals every cripple, every ill child.

He then seats Himself and begins to teach. After a time, He picks up a little one who has timidly come up to Him. She leans against the breast of Christ and goes to sleep. Jesus makes room on His lap for a second little one—perhaps a blind boy He has just healed. The child, filled with wonder, looks intently at the kindly face of Jesus.

Jesus pauses, and several delighted children begin to sing. Others join them. Soon "Hosanna to the Son of David" fills the temple court (Matthew 21:14-16).

Two scenes. In one, at the administrative center of the universe, you gaze out on clusters and superclusters of galaxies. In the other, on a tiny rebel planet, you watch as an Intergalactic Executive from that center tenderly holds two children on His lap. How could anyone not love this great Man?

Personality plus!

When teaching religion classes at Andrews University, I sometimes ask, "What one personality trait in Jesus Christ do you most admire?" I then have a student go to the chalkboard and record the qualities the class suggests. Generally, the traits suggested fill the entire board!

"Think of the kindest, strongest, most generous, and appealing person you have ever known," Norval Pease once wrote. "Then in your imagination magnify, purify, and enrich that individual a thousand times. Even so, you have not even begun to imagine what Jesus is like" (Norval Pease, "What Jesus Can Do for You," *These Times*, Aug., 1981, p. 16).

Employ thousands of gifted writers and artists to work full time. Ask them to picture the matchless attractions of Jesus. They would never exhaust the subject!

A cause for amazed admiration

Nearly 600 years before the birth of Christ, Isaiah attempted to describe the coming Savior. "His name shall be called Wonderful," he began (Isaiah 9:6, KJV).

The word *wonderful* means "full of wonder"—a reason for astonishment, a cause for amazed admiration, something beyond anything previously known.

A reason for astonishment. An intergalactic Executive comes to this planet as a baby born in a smelly stable!

Cause for amazed admiration. He speaks worlds and galaxies into existence "with the breath of his mouth" (Psalm 33:6). He puts awesome power within the atom! He guides clusters and superclusters of galaxies on their sweep through space! Yet He has a heart that longs to save every sinner.

Something beyond anything previously known. As I associate with high school age youth, I notice this: most of them rate friends according to personality. They want companions who are friendly, outgoing, enjoyable to be with. Jesus is all that—a thousand times over.

The rugged seventeen-year-old who worked in a carpenter shop was also the co-Creator of hundreds of billions of galaxies. Today He has everything—personality, wealth, power, skill, generosity, love.

Where could you possibly find a better friend?

Notes

1. Paul W. Hodge, *Galaxies* (Cambridge: Harvard University Press, 1986), p. 2.

2. *Collier's Encyclopedia* (New York: Macmillan Educational Company, 1987), vol. 7, article "Constellations," p. 226.

CHAPTER FOUR

Why I Love Being a Christian

I love being a Christian!" Bob Beltz exclaims in *Transforming Your Prayer Life*. "It is the ultimate no-lose proposition."

He explains that in just about every area of life, success is measured by performance. A person's athletic value depends on performance. Success in school comes from performance. A pastor's success or failure largely depends upon performance.

"Becoming a Christian is the one experience in my life that was not based on my performance," he says. "I became a Christian on the basis of my failure and Jesus Christ's performance."[1]

Jesus Christ's performance in place of my failure!

Words about Jesus are so inadequate! In trying to describe His personality, I rewrote and refined parts of the previous chapter at least a dozen times. Those attempts made Him all the more precious. I would love Him even if He didn't offer a "no-lose proposition." I want to serve Him, not for benefits, but from appreciation and love.

41

At the same time, I am grateful for every benefit. As I journaled this morning, I jotted down a few of the many reasons why I, too, love being a Christian:

- The simplicity of God's plan for saving sinners.

- Christ's eagerness to forgive my sins.

- The freedom I have found in Christ.

- The fact that God loves me unconditionally; He loves me with a love *not* based on my performance.

I grew up in a non-church family—no grace at meals, no Bible study, no discussion of religion. In my early teens I wondered if a God even existed.

We lived on a farm in northern Oklahoma. I watched apple trees blossom. I helped plant and care for the family garden. On cool summer mornings I carried watermelons to the family cellar—then helped eat crisp slices of red melon in the shade of the house on hot afternoons. I listened to meadowlarks as they sang from atop fence posts. I watched the Oklahoma sunrises and sunsets.

On the hot summer evenings, our family usually sat together out on the porch steps until bedtime. In that rural setting, we got spectacular views of the Milky Way as it arced across the sky. I decided that there must be a God.

My first Bible

I attended high school in Newkirk, Oklahoma. One day while going past the dime store in that small town, I noticed a New Testament in the window. I bought one and began reading it. About that time Bob and Don, my two younger brothers, started getting letters from California that contained Voice of Prophecy Bible lessons. (Years later we learned that the teacher in their one-room grade school, a former Seventh-day Adventist, had enrolled all her upper grade students in the junior Bible course.)

Their lessons fascinated me. I enrolled in the senior course.

Additional providences enabled me to be baptized into the Seventh-day Adventist Church shortly before I was eighteen. Later, both Bob and Don and our younger sister Betty also joined the church. All of us praise God for the beautiful truths those lessons brought into our lives.

I still have most of the thirty-six lessons in the Bible course I took. Lesson four asked, "What Must I Do to Be Saved?" Lesson five carried the title "Repentance, Confession, Forgiveness."

God's simple plan for saving sinners

The opening paragraphs in the lesson about repentance and forgiveness said this:

> "The matter of becoming converted—becoming a Christian—is not so complicated as Satan would like people to think. . . . It does not take high-sounding philosophy and involved theology to make a Christian out of a sinner. It takes just simple faith in Jesus" (p. 1).

As I teach young people about Christ, I try to show the simplicity of that faith by telling them, "Saving faith is a *transaction*. In a transaction you give something, and you get something."

I then have them open their Bibles to this statement of Paul: "God made him who had no sin to be sin for us, so that in him we might become the righteousness of God" (2 Corinthians 5:21).

At this point I ask, "Does anyone have an ordinary lead pencil that you would exchange for a $5 bill?"

Someone gives me a pencil, and I hand him or her the $5 bill. I then ask the class, "What just happened?"

After a student identifies it as an exchange, a transaction, I draw two lessons:

■ The transaction that makes one a Christian is simple. You give Christ the only thing you have to give—a sinful life. In return, He gives you His righteousness.

■ The exchange must be total. The student gave the *entire* pencil. So it is in becoming a Christian. "You will seek me and find me," God says, "when you seek me with all your heart" (Jeremiah 29:13).

Saving faith is a transaction. You give Christ the only thing you have to give—a sinful heart. In return, He gives you His righteousness.

Totally forgiven

The Bible lesson about repentance and forgiveness asked, "Are some sins too dark to be forgiven?"

The lesson cited this promise: "Come now, let us reason together, says the Lord. Though your sins are like scarlet, they shall be as white as snow; though they are red as crimson, they shall be like wool" (Isaiah 1:18).

The radio mail of the Voice of Prophecy, the lesson said, brings the following kind of appeal more often than all others:

> "I've gone so far in sin that God can't possibly save me. I knew I was doing wrong. And now I've tried to come back to Him, but I keep remembering my sins. I pray, and my prayers are not heard. There is no use for me to try any more. Do you think there is any hope at all that God could still save me?"

Have you ever had similar feelings? Do your sins seem like a wall between you and God? The lesson suggested, "To these broken, suffering hearts should be held out the sure promises of God's Word. Forgiveness is awaiting *every repentant sinner and every repentant backslider."*

Here's the promise: "If we confess our sins, he is faithful and just and will forgive us our sins and purify us from all unrighteousness" (1 John 1:9).

I love that promise! As we admit our need, as we confess our sins, God freely forgives. And He does more than that: the promise says that He also *purifies* us. As we look to Jesus, as we study His life, we become more and more like Him.

Repentance is a gift

Another salvation promise says: "God exalted him to his own right hand as Prince and Savior that he might give repentance and forgiveness to Israel" (Acts 5:31).

Even repentance is a gift! When I ask for repentance, there is one thing I can do: I can *choose* to think about Jesus dying on the cross for me. I may not even *feel* like repenting. But I can open my Bible to the story of Christ being crucified and ask myself, "Why this sacrifice?"

As I think about the crucifixion, Jesus fulfills this promise: "And I, if I be lifted up from the earth, will draw all men unto me" (John 12:32, KJV).

When I then see my need and confess my sins, I am *totally forgiven.* I am accepted just as if I had never sinned. When students find this hard to believe, I take them back to this promise: *"God made him who had no sin to be sin for us, so that in him we might become the righteousness of God"* (2 Corinthians 5:21).

Freedom: another gift

The "everlasting gospel" (Revelation 14:6, KJV) offers more than forgiveness. Jesus said: "You will know the truth, and the truth will set you free" (John 8:32).

I still remember thinking about that verse as I worked one morning on the Oklahoma farm where I grew up. I had taken a Voice of Prophecy lesson along as I took a team and wagon out to get firewood. I read that promise as I went across the pasture. I knew it described what was happening in my life.

When Jesus talked about truth bringing freedom, some of His listeners didn't like what they heard. They shot back, "We are Abraham's descendants and have never been slaves of anyone. How can you say that we shall be set free?" (John 8:33).

Jesus replied, "I tell you the truth, everyone who sins is a slave to sin" (John 8:34).

Not everyone recognizes sin as slavery—at least not at first. Satan comes to us and says the same thing he told the prodigal son, "Let me tell you how to be free. Forget God's law. Forget the restrictions of religion. Let me show you how to really live."

That son found entertainment. He found bright lights and loud music and prostitutes. But not freedom and happiness.

The Bible describes his "find" in these words: "The evil deeds of a wicked man ensnare him; the cords of his sin hold him fast" (Proverbs 5:22).

It was through repentance and confession that the prodigal found real freedom. He started toward it when he said, "I will set out and go back to my father and say to him: Father, I have sinned against heaven and against you. I am no longer worthy to be called your son; make me like one of your hired men" (Luke 15:18, 19).

The father gladly welcomed his returning son. He clothed him with "the best robe." He called for a celebration, exclaiming, "This son of mine was dead and is alive again; he was lost and is found." (Luke 15:24).

There's no freedom like the freedom of being unconditionally loved and totally forgiven! That's real freedom! "If the Son sets you free, you will be free indeed" (John 8:36).

Loved before you change

During the Dark Ages many people thought that they had to *earn* God's favor—that you gained merit by good works. Then, through Martin Luther and other Protestant reformers, the Bible teaching of righteousness by faith began to be restored. Millions still think that they must earn at least part of their standing with God. They find it

"I was exhausted by the constant feeling of never quite measuring up."

hard to believe that God loves them unconditionally—that He loves them *before* they make changes

In his book *Enjoying God*, Lloyd John Ogilvie suggested that for many, the statement "You are loved now" is almost impossible to believe. He tells what we tend to think:

> *"Someday, maybe. . . . Sometime when we get our act together, shape up our personalities and get rid of our bad habits or wandering nonpublic thoughts and fantasies—perhaps then. But certainly not now."*

> "Fears and memories lead us to think, *If you knew about me you wouldn't say that. Surely there's something I must do to earn that kind of grace, like make amends or perform some kind of penance."*[2]

Dr. Ogilvie then shared an experience he'd had while attending the University of Edinburgh: "Because of financial pressures I had to accordion my studies into a shorter than usual period. Carrying a double load was very demanding, and I was exhausted by the constant feeling of never quite measuring up. Sadly, I was not living the truths I was studying . . . ."

A constant feeling of never quite measuring up!

Then one of Ogilvie's professors stopped him in the hall. "He looked me in the eyes intensely," he said. "Then he smiled warmly, took my coat lapels in his hands, drew me down a few inches from his face, and said, 'Dear boy, you are loved now!'"

You are loved now! "I think of these words every day," said Ogilvie,[3] "sometimes every hour."

At times just about every Christian is tempted to think, "I've got to perform to be accepted. I must reach a certain standard in order to be loved."

The eternal gospel does not demand, "*Do* and you will be accepted; *perform* and you will be loved." Instead, it declares, *You are loved now!*

The same gospel then works to transform us from within. By beholding Christ, we become more and more like Him (2 Corinthins 3:18).

He gives us the power needed to change our lives. At every step, from the beginning to the final touches, we are continuously loved.

That's righteousness by faith!

And that, in my estimation, is the greatest of all reasons for being enthusiastic about Christ!

Notes

1. Bob Beltz, *Transforming Your Prayer Life* (Dallas, Tex.: Word, Inc., 1993), pp. 105, 106. Used by permission.

2. Lloyd John Ogilvie, adapted from *Enjoying God* (Dallas, Tex.: Word, Inc., 1989).

3. Ibid.

CHAPTER FIVE

"Teach Us to Pray"

Let's look in upon a scene recorded in Luke 11:

The time: probably an early spring morning in A.D. 30, about a year before the crucifixion.

The place: a secluded spot, possibly near Bethany, where Jesus has gone to pray. Mentally picture the kneeling Christ. Sense the freshness of a Palestine springtime— green grass, wildflowers that sparkle with dew, perhaps an apricot tree in bloom.

The action: Jesus is praying aloud. The disciples have just found Him, after a brief absence. He continues talking to God—seemingly unaware that twelve men are watching and listening. He prays as if in the actual presence of His Father.

The reaction: As they listen, the disciples wish they could pray like Jesus does. They wait until Christ says, "Amen." Then they exclaim, "Lord, teach us to pray" (Luke 11:1).

Some months earlier, in the Sermon on the Mount, Christ had talked about prayer (Matthew 6:5-15). He had urged that:

1. Private prayer should be **secret**—it should not be done

"on street corners to be seen of men" (v. 5). When you want to pray, He suggested, "go into your room, close the door, and pray to your Father, who sees what is done in secret" (v. 6).

2. Prayer should be **short**—right to the point. "When you pray," He said, "do not keep on babbling like the pagans, who think they will be heard because of their many words" (v. 7).

3. Prayer should be **sincere**—in a forgiving spirit. "If you forgive men when they sin against you," Jesus said, "your heavenly Father will also forgive you" (v. 14).

At that time Christ had given a model prayer—brief, yet comprehensive—that we call "the Lord's Prayer" (Matthew 6:9-13). In Luke 11, Christ again gave the same prayer.

Here in Luke, He told a story about a man who had unexpected company at midnight. His cupboards were empty, and he went to a neighbor to borrow three loaves

---

God isn't like people who "don't want to be bothered." He loves being "bothered." He delights to give.

---

of bread. The neighbor, understandably, didn't appreciate a midnight interruption.

The man with company kept knocking and finally got the needed bread. Jesus drew a lesson: ask, seek, knock. Those who ask will receive. Seekers will find. Doors will open to those who knock.

He then used short illustrations about the willingness of fathers to give (Luke 11:5-10). God isn't like the "I-don't-want-to-be-bothered-at-midnight" neighbor. He apprecates being "bothered," and He delights to give.

Christ concluded His prayer remarks with this suggestion:

> "If you, then, though you are evil, know how to
> give good gifts to your children, how much more

will your Father give the Holy Spirit to those
who ask him" (Luke 11:13).

Note the *"your* Father." Consider also God's eagerness to
give His Spirit to His children. That Gift prepares the way
for all other gifts. With the confidence of a child, we may
ask for the Holy Spirit to guide us in our daily experiences.

Matthew 6 contains a similar focus on God as a Father.
Christ deals there with these subjects: prayer, giving,
fasting, and trusting God for food and clothes. Within that
context, He spoke of God as Father *twelve times.*

That's twelve times in just that one chapter!

A new idea

Calling God "Father" was a new idea to Christ's followers. In the Old Testament, God is occasionally spoken of
as a Father (Psalm 103:13; Isaiah 63:16). But in Old
Testament prayers no one addresses Him that way. Even
in the Psalms, David never greets God as Father.

In the gospels, however, Jesus encourages us to come

When a believer asks for God's favor or blessing, his
or her requests are "music in His ears"!

---

to God like a little child. He wants us to come eagerly—the
way a child runs to meet daddy as he comes home from
work.

The author of *Christ's Object Lessons* points out that Christ
gives us the privilege of addressing God as Father, and adds:

> "This name, spoken to Him and of Him, is a sign
> of our love and trust toward Him, and a pledge
> of His regard and relationship to us. Spoken
> when asking His favor or blessing, it is as music
> in His ears. That we might not think it presump-

tion to call Him by this name, He repeated it
again and again" (pp. 141, 142).

That's almost beyond belief! When I call God "Father,"
my requests are "music in His ears"! They make His day!
Believing that adds an awesome sense of wonder to "the
privilege of prayer"!

Perhaps you come from such a background that the
word "father" does not awaken tender feelings. Don't let
that dampen your enthusiasm for God as a Father. While
all human fathers are imperfect, God isn't! Think again of
the temple cleansing scene as described in Matthew
21:12-17. After cleansing the temple, Jesus heals the
sick—adults and children alike. He then seats Himself to
teach. Children crowd around Him and lift their voices in
song. Jesus receives the affectionate kisses of the little ones
He has healed.

Your heavenly Father is just as tender!

Teaching—and learning—about prayer

As I prepared this chapter, I reviewed things I have
learned from nearly twenty years of teaching college and
seminary students about faith and prayer. I have found it
a lot easier to teach about prayer than actually to pray. I'm
still working on that inconsistency.

Here are a few more things I have learned:

**1. A lot of us practice prayer more as a duty than as a
delightful pleasure.**

I have made daily prayer enough of a habit that it's hard
to get into bed without kneeling to pray. But too often my
bedtime prayers have been "duty" prayers. It's sort of like
brushing my teeth—something I do to keep my conscience
from bothering me.

2. To be effective, prayer must be mingled with faith.

I am learning to pray with an increasingly strong
conviction that God "is able" (Ephesians 3:20). As Gabriel
told Mary, "Nothing is impossible with God" (Luke 1:37).

3. I have learned that prayer is a "science"—it's governed by laws, by "conditions."

I've had a lot of unanswered prayers—or, to be more exact, a lot of prayers to which God said No. In due time I usually learn that my request was denied for one of two reasons: (a) I did not meet the conditions, or (b) it would not have been for my best good.

4. I've discovered that the Bible contains promises applicable to every possible human need.

The Bible is intensely practical! In it I find advice and promises for my physical needs: health, finances, clothing, food. It offers help for my spiritual problems: salvation, forgiveness, increase of faith—and much, much more. Whatever the need—loneliness, bereavement, temptation, emergencies, a crisis—there is a helpful promise!

5. My wife and I have repeatedly seen faith and prayer put the "hedge" of Job 1:10 about our three children and about young people entrusted to our care.

During the fourteen years my wife and I were at Glendale Adventist Academy, we sponsored a hiking and camping club. We chose Psalm 121 as a "Camping Club Psalm"—asking God to preserve our "going out" and our "coming in."

He did. We took students on more than sixty major outings—to the top of Mt. Whitney, to the bottom of the Grand Canyon, on ten-day pack trips in the High Sierras, snow skiing, water skiing, and so on. Groups ranged in size from one carload up to eighty youth—other people's children for whose safety we were responsible. We shall be forever grateful for God's care over us on those excursions.

6. I am learning to pray with an awareness that I am speaking to a Friend who possesses perfect skills, immense wealth, and unlimited power.

Among men—whatever the emergency or the need—we want skilled help. We also want adequate power and resources to be available. God has unlimited supplies of all three!

7. I find that reading from the Bible before I pray and using it as I pray adds newness and variety to my prayer times.

The Bible contains much "subject matter for prayer"—especially in the gospels, the epistles, Acts, Isaiah, and many other areas. Currently I am "praying through the Psalms" by reading one Psalm each day and then talking to God about its content.

8. When I consistently praise God, I have more bestowed for which to praise Him.

You may want to test this over a period of several weeks! Thank God for the many blessings already received. And try thanking Him for what He is *going to do!* See if a spirit of praise doesn't increase the blessings received.

9. I am finding that devotional study before prayer can be an adventure in which I often discover new insights.

On each journal page I use a part of it for that day's "Something New" discovery. Almost every day I record some new insight I discover from my study of the Bible. Often these discoveries become subject matter for prayer and for praise.

"Something new"

A parable in Matthew 13 helped me start a "something new" habit. Jesus had shared a group of parables in what we now call "the sermon by the sea." After seven parables—the sower, the tares, the mustard seed, and others—He asked His disciples, "Do you understand these things?" (Matthew 13:51, TEV).

They answered, "Yes." Jesus then concluded His sermon with this illustration:

> "This means, then, that every teacher of the Law
> who becomes a disciple in the Kingdom of
> Heaven is like a homeowner who takes new and
> old things out of the storage room" (Matthew
> 13:52, TEV).

Consider this interpretation: The homeowner is the believer, and the storage room is the Bible. The "old" would be truths already known. The "new" would be new insights.

My Workshop in Prayer students read about ninety pages from a devotional book entitled *My Life Today.* A comment related to God's "unsearchable riches" (Romans 11:33) suggests: "Every day you should learn something new from the Scripture" (p. 22).

This "something new" generally won't be new interpretations of doctrine or prophecy. I see it, rather, as new insights, often from familiar passages, that help apply those truths in practical ways to daily life.

Recent "something new" discoveries

Last summer I was asked to prepare a short nature talk for a Lake Michigan beach vespers. I focused on Jesus as the Light of the World. As a text, I selected this statement:

> "When Jesus spoke again to the people, he said,
> 'I am the light of the world. Whoever follows
> me will never walk in darkness, but will have the
> light of life'" (John 8:12).

For the first time I noticed the word *again.* That connects John 8:12 to the previous verse. There Jesus had told the young woman caught in adultery, "Neither do I condemn you. Go now and leave your life of sin" (John 8:11). Or, as the KJV words it, "Go, and sin no more." The very next thing He talked about was following Him as "the light of life."

My new insight? *Choosing Jesus as "the light of life" enables us to say "No" to temptation and sin.*

Shortly thereafter, it dawned on me that the first promise in the Old Testament, Genesis 3:15, and the first promise in the New Testament, Matthew 1:21, both deal with salvation from sin.

In the former, God announced His purpose to put "enmity" between His children and Satan. "I will help you to hate sin," He promised. And in Matthew 1:21 Gabriel told Joseph that Mary would give birth to a Son who should be called Jesus, for "He will save his people from their sins." God promises salvation, not *in* sin, but *from* sin.

Insights that deal with daily life

Unless you know your Bible quite well, you probably will find something new almost every time you read it. If you are well acquainted with God's Word, a delightful way to gain new insights is to read from alternate versions. One of my favorites is the *Today's English Version* published by the American Bible Society.

I am amazed at how often the Bible speaks directly to me. Here are examples:

■ You have heard the saying that "haste makes waste." The King James of Proverbs 19:2 says something similar: "He that hastest with his feet sinneth." The TEV pointedly puts it: "Impatience will get you into trouble."

■ In the Kings James, Proverbs 12:1 says, "Whoso loveth instruction loveth knowledge: but he that hateth reproof is brutish." The TEV is unmistakably clear: "Anyone who loves knowledge wants to be told when he is wrong. It is stupid to hate being corrected."

Such statements are worded so plainly that I have no trouble getting the point.

Exuberant gratitude

I recently found this suggestion in a Bible commentary: Psalm 103 and Psalm 104 are "exuberant" in tone. Psalm 103 is a psalm of gratitude for God's compassion and grace, while Psalm 104 expresses delight in the works of God's creation. After rereading Psalms 103 and 104, I wrote this as a new insight: *These two psalms alone are reason for exuberant gratitude to God.*

Gratitude and praise are especially prominent in the Psalms. Here's a "something new" idea I found in the Living

Bible: "Arise, O harp and lyre! Let us greet the dawn with a song" (Psalm 57:8).

Even a cloudy morning can be greeted with a song. Read Psalm 103 or 104 the next time the weather depresses you. You'll find reason for praise even during miserable weather!

Usable ideas

As you think about possible "usable ideas" that you could draw from this chapter, consider these options:

1. Spend some time studying Luke 11:1-13. Look for ideas in this passage that you could use. If you have a Bible with marginal references, check some of those for possible new insights.

2. If you have access to the book *Christ's Object Lessons*, read the chapter entitled "Asking to Give." It is commentary about the Luke 11:1-13 passage we examined at the start of this chapter. Here is a sample of the "usable ideas" that chapter contains:

> "Talk and act as if your faith were invincible. The Lord is rich in resources; He owns the world. Look heavenward in faith. Look to Him who has light and power and efficiency" (p. 147).

3. Begin making it a habit, as Psalm 57:8 in the Living Bible suggests, to "greet the dawn with a song." (Getting to bed at a reasonable hour helps!)

4. Try praying through several psalms. Prayerfully read a psalm and then talk to God about some of the ideas you find there.

5. Look for "something new" insights as you read your Bible. Underline or write out those you want to remember. As a start, try Proverbs or a Gospel in a paraphrase or a modern-speech version.

CHAPTER SIX

My First "Whatever It Takes" Praying

My physician's nurse called this morning to give me the results of a cholesterol test I took yesterday. "Whatever you're doing," she exclaimed, "keep doing it!"

My annual physical six weeks earlier indicated a cholesterol level of 230. Previously I had read a book entitled *To Your Health*. The author, Dr. Hans Diehl, had suggested that anyone who keeps his cholesterol level below 150 probably will never have a heart attack or a stroke.

My 230 level demanded some changes! At the least I needed to get it down under 200.

I saw it as a "whatever it takes" challenge! Prayer alone obviously would not be enough. The praying would need some "whatever it takes" lifestyle changes!

I hadn't used flesh foods for decades. And about three years earlier I had also dropped the use of eggs and dairy products. But, at least in my case, that wasn't enough. I now made further changes—elimination of most fat. This included most vegetarian meats, many of which are very high in fat.

I also started getting more exercise. After six weeks, I had my cholesterol checked again. It was down to 127!

This experience illustrates an important truth about "whatever it takes" praying: for maximum results, such praying needs to be accompanied with "whatever it takes" living.

Prayer combined with human effort

The defeat of the Amalekites, as recorded in Exodus 17:8-16, illustrates the relationship between prayer and doing our part.

The Amalakites, a fierce and warlike tribe, made an unprovoked attack upon the Hebrews as they traveled toward Sinai. Their first victims were the faint and weary ones who had fallen behind. Moses knew that his people were not ready for the life-or-death struggle.

That evening Moses and other leaders met for counsel and prayer. The plan they developed was this:

■ Joshua would choose a body of soldiers from the varied tribes. The next morning he and his men would go out to engage the attackers.

■ Moses would stand on a nearby hill and pray for the Israeli troops (Ex. 17:9, 10). They would do what they could and depend on God to do the rest.

The next morning Joshua and his troops marched out to battle. Moses, with Aaron and Hur, took a position on a hill overlooking the battlefield. With arms stretched heavenward, he prayed for the armies of Israel.

While Moses' hands were up the Israelis advanced. But when fatigue caused him to lower his arms, Amalek prevailed. Aaron and Hur noticed this. They strode over to Moses and held up his hands until the Hebrew troops repulsed the attackers.

This story illustrates two truths:

1. Doing our part: Moses did not ask God to overcome the Amalekites while Israel did nothing. He sent out Joshua and his troops to do everything they could.

2. Dependence upon God: Moses did not depend on human skill alone. He pleaded with God to bless Joshua and his troops.

That combination gets results!

Starting "whatever it takes" praying

Do you remember the Chapter 1 story about a dying pastor who told his son to do "whatever it takes" to win people to Christ? That illustration suggested an idea to me. Why not start a "whatever it takes" prayer list?

I began such a list in July of 1989. With each request I also included a reference to an appropriate Bible promise.

I had made prayer lists before. But until July of 1989, I had never developed a "whatever it takes" list. I began with several personal needs. In my first two requests I invited the Lord to do whatever it takes to:

1. Help me experience a daily reconversion.

2. Help me make any needed lifestyle changes.

God has been working with me on both. I still have a long way to go, but I am grateful for God's patience as He nudges me along. I continue to bring these petitions to Him. The more I pray with a "whatever it takes" spirit, the more He seems able to do.

Other requests

Another personal request had to do with finances. From 1977 through mid-1984, I had done editorial work on religion texts. After completing that task I had chosen self-employment as a freelance writer. Income was both uncertain and limited. In July of 1989 I began praying that, if it were God's will, I might start getting a regular income.

Along with praying, I made inquiries about possible teaching or pastoral openings that might not require moving. During the summer of 1990, the pastor of a nearby district accepted an invitation to serve in another part of the country. That created an opening for a pastor in that two-church district near Andrews University.

Thus, since August of 1990, I have pastored the Coloma and the Eau Claire, Michigan, SDA churches—the former at that time having a book membership of 69 and the latter of 180.

As another "whatever it takes" request, I began praying for Seventh-day Adventist leadership—especially at the General Conference level. At first I prayed for them collectively, but more recently I have been praying for several leaders by name.

My first "whatever it takes" requests also included prayers for several pastors and leaders in other communions and for leaders in organizations such as "Focus on the Family"—leaders I think of as part of our "extended Christian fellowship."

I especially rely on the following part of Genesis 12:2 when praying for both secular and Christian leaders: "I will bless you . . . and you will be a blessing." God first gave this assurance to Abraham, but I see it as needed by all leaders.

Here's another promise I use almost every day in my prayers for leaders: "The path of the righteous is like the first gleam of dawn, shining ever brighter till the full light of day" (Proverbs 4:18).

My almost daily prayer is that God will do "whatever it takes" to fulfill the preceding promises for every truth-loving pastor and leader in every denomination and in secular society.

WIT and praying for large groups

Until recently I didn't see much value in praying collectively for large groups or for an entire denomination. Then I came across the following two statements about God knowing the name of each star:

> "He determines the number of the stars and calls
> them each by name, Great is our Lord and
> mighty in power; his understanding has no limit"
> (Psalm 147:4, 5).

"He . . . brings out the starry host one by one,
and calls them each by name. Because of his
great power and mighty strength, not one of
them is missing" (Isaiah 40:26).

That's awesome! God calls each star by name! That's at
least 100 billion stars just in our home-town Milky Way!

These two statements gave me new glimpses of God's
amazing mental capability. I won't frustrate Him if I pray
collectively for every believer in my denomination. Nor is
He overwhelmed if I collectively pray for every Christian
in the entire world.

In Chapter 2 we noted that in praying for his people,
Nehemiah used "arguments" drawn from Scripture. I use
the above two Bible statements the same way. My prayer
might go like this:

"Dear Father, in Isaiah 40:26 you say that you call each
star by name. With that kind of knowledge, it's nothing
for You to send the Holy Spirit at this very moment to
believers everywhere. Bless each this very day and make
each a blessing."

I love to pray like this on clear nights when I am out
under the stars. In the winter I especially like to pray as I
gaze up toward Orion.

It's true that with this kind of generality you can't tell if
your prayer is answered. I don't worry about that. I trust
my God. If every word I speak is recorded by angels, as
Jesus indicates in Matthew 12:35-37, it's likely that every
sincere prayer is also recorded. And if it is, perhaps the
influence that prayer has had for good is recorded. If so,
in eternity believers may have opportunity to see the
influence of their general prayers.

Praying for other lands

Most of my 1989 "whatever it takes" requests had to do
with the progress of the gospel in various sections of the
world. Specific countries I put on my list included Communist lands such as Cuba, the Soviet Union, and mainland

China. I began praying that God would do "whatever it takes" to open doors for the gospel in these lands.

The Kneeling Christian, a book written by an anonymous Christian in the early part of this century, cites evidence that praying for specific countries can produce conversions there. The author points out that "we can bring down showers of blessing upon India or Africa or China just as readily as we can get the few drops needed for our own little plot" (pp. 32, 33).

For decades thousands of Christians of all faiths have been praying for the hundreds of millions of people dominated by Communism. Those prayers are now beginning to be answered.

A book by Mark Finley entitled *The Cross and the Kremlin* tells the story of the evangelistic meetings Mark held in the Kremlin in the spring of 1992. There's a great hunger for the gospel in Moscow and throughout the former Soviet Union. Never in history have so many doors opened so swiftly as in Russia and the other republics of that vast land. More on this in the next chapter.

Praying for your pastor

The Bible puts a lot of emphasis on Christians praying for each other and for their pastors and leaders. Bible examples include the church praying for Peter (Acts 12), Paul for his converts (Colossians 1:9-14), and Jesus for all of His followers (John 17:20, 21). Paul asked the believers at Thessalonicia to pray for him and Timothy—"that the message of the Lord may spread rapidly and be honored" (2 Thessalonians 3:1, 2).

In both of my churches I have members who tell me, "I'm praying for you every day." In my *Faith and Prayer* syllabus I included the following comment made to Seventh-day Adventist believers back in 1881:

> "Happy the minister who has a faithful Aaron and Hur to strengthen his hands when they become weary and to hold them up by faith and prayer. Such a support is a powerful aid to the

servant of Christ in his work and will often make
the cause of truth to triumph gloriously" (*Testimonies for the Church*, vol. 4, p. 531).

Glorious triumphs! We are seeing amazing providences
in formerly Communist lands. Let's pray that God will use
pastors and others to help bring about a similar break-
through in North America!

In July 1989, I included the name of my own pastor on
my WIT list. At that time my wife and I attended the
Pioneer Memorial Church at Andrews University. Since
1983, the senior pastor of that 3,000-member congregation
has been Dwight K. Nelson. I have especially appreciated
his efforts to bring revival to the Andrews campus.

Even though I am no longer a member there, I continue
to pray that God will bless Pastor Dwight as he seeks
renewal and revival at Andrews University. With students
from eighty nations on campus at any given time, a revival
at Andrews will have an influence all over the world.

In *Prayer Shield*, a 1992 book about praying for pastors,
Peter Wagner tells of a pastor in Argentina who asks his
church members and families to pray for him when saying
grace at meals.

If you aren't already doing so, and if you have a prayer
list, why not include your pastor? Let him know that you
are praying for him. And expect God to bless.

Dependence upon God

In my "whatever it takes" praying, I am learning to
depend upon God far more than upon anything that I or
my members can do. Jesus spoke plainly when He cau-
tioned, "Apart from me you can do nothing" (John 15:5).
Within the context of John 14-16, Jesus talked again and
again about the work of the Holy Spirit.

This seems to suggest that *the very first lesson to be learned
is dependence upon God*. Without the presence of the Holy
Spirit we can accomplish nothing.

Consider also this related caution: A "whatever it takes" spirit should not lead us to a violation of the laws of health through overwork. Nor should it lead to neglecting one's family.

Within my human limitations I want to do whatever I

The very first lesson to be learned is that of dependence upon God.

---

can to reclaim non-attending members. I want to do all I can to secure new interests. But I also depend largely upon what God can do. I have been especially drawn to this promise: "Are not all angels ministering spirits sent to serve those who will inherit salvation?" (Hebrews 1:14).

Praying during the day

I am developing the habit of praying short WIT petitions as I go through the day. I write out my WIT requests in my journal during my morning devotional time. Then I generally take the page with these requests out of my journal, fold it, and put it into my shirt pocket. If I limit myself to three or four requests, later glances at the list help me memorize them.

Throughout the rest of the day I often include Hebrews 1:14 with my WIT prayers. Not a day goes by without my asking God to use angels to minister to those on my prayer list and to Christians in various countries.

I find many reminders to breathe a WIT prayer as I go through the day. While I was writing this chapter, a Rose of Sharon tree with mostly white blossoms bloomed continuously outside my office window. As I typed, I would often glance at it. During that pause I would pray that God would do "whatever it takes" to give the children and youth in my congregations a similar beauty.

For me, God's creative power has become a reminder of His recreative power. Fruit trees in bloom, flowers about the yard or in a park, the song of birds, changing cloud formations, the laughter of children—all can become invitations to breathe a WIT prayer.

One pastor suggests sending a prayer to heaven each hour on the hour. For those in school, the ringing of a bell for class dismissal could be a reminder to pray. Stopping at red lights can give a pause for a WIT petition. I am making it a habit, when saying grace, to include a "whatever it takes" for that day's written list of WIT petitions.

Do quick prayers help?

Do you wonder if such quick, simple prayers make any difference?

In his book *Prevailing Prayer*, Taylor G. Bunch noted that many Bible prayers were very short. The publican of Luke 18 simply prayed "God, have mercy on me, a sinner" (v. 13). The Syrophoenician woman got an answer when she prayed, "Lord, help me." And Peter got help just by praying, "Lord, save me." Wrote Bunch:

> "The prophets of Baal prayed long and loud, but
> . . . there was no answer to their wailing cries
> and weird incantations. All day long they begged
> their false gods to hear and answer their petition.
> Elijah was calm and quiet, and his prayer was
> short. It is recorded in two verses of sixty-three
> words . . . but it was a prevailing prayer. It com-
> pletely changed the situation and saved the na-
> tion of Israel from idolatry and doubtless from
> complete destruction."[1]

Review the experience of Nehemiah, as recorded in Nehemiah 2:1-4. King Artaxerxes had asked Nehemiah, "What is it that you want?" Before Nehemiah answered, he "prayed to the God of heaven" (v. 4).

In that brief prayer, did Nehemiah bow his head? Probably not. Did he close his eyes? Probably not. Did he pray aloud? Hardly. Yet God heard and answered.

There is no magical power in "whatever it takes" or in any other wording. But doesn't Nehemiah 2 indicate that a very brief prayer can change the course of history?

Could it be that your "whatever it takes" prayers could have a similar influence?

A little-used resource

I believe that silent, "whatever it takes" praying is perhaps the greatest yet-to-be-tapped reservoir of spiritual power in the church today. We breathe a prayer as we come and go, and it reaches the administrative center of the universe. It is God to whom we speak; that prayer is heard.

Let's imagine that a million believers become convinced that WIT petitions can make a decided difference. Suppose each of us were to include countries such as Cuba, Communist China, and North Korea on a WIT prayer list. Many times a day a million of us send a WIT petition heavenward. Could those prayers give God the right to work with unprecedented power in those lands?

I know from personal experience that "whatever it takes" praying has a life-changing effect on the petitioner. It influences how one uses time and money. It intensifies one's love and concern for people.

Testing the idea

Would you like to test the WIT prayer idea? Here are several suggestions:

1. Start a daily WIT prayer list of some kind, using a notebook or small booklet. Begin with personal and family needs. Include, also, your pastor. (Perhaps, as mentioned earlier in this chapter, you could also say a sentence prayer for your pastor each time you say grace.)

2. Begin to pray for specific countries such as Cuba and Communist China. Ask God to do whatever it takes to open doors there.

3. Ask God to do whatever it takes to bring renewal and revival in North America and in other Western countries.

4. Cultivate the habit of sending a "whatever it takes" prayer up to God many times during the day. Feel free, sometimes, to abbreviate it to just three words: *Whatever it takes.*

Notes:

1. Taylor G. Bunch, Prevailing Prayer (Washington, D.C.: Review and Herald Publishing Association, 1946 [reproduced in 1993]), p. 107.

CHAPTER SEVEN

Whatever It Takes Praying and Berlin Walls

The fall of the Berlin Wall in December of 1989 started what one newspaper called "the century's greatest drama"—the disintegration of the Soviet Union. By the end of December, 1991, that mighty Communist nation had ceased to exist.

This dissolution took place with incredible swiftness—and doors for proclaiming the gospel opened just as rapidly. Back in 1989, who would have dreamed, for example, that by the spring of 1992 Seventh-day Adventists would be conducting evangelistic meetings right within the 280-acre Kremlin complex?

These meetings were held in the Congress Hall—a beautiful 6,000-seat auditorium that had served as a center for atheistic propaganda. During the last two weeks of March, 1992, double sessions each day brought 12,000 Russians to the Congress Hall to hear the gospel of Jesus Christ preached by Mark Finley, speaker-director for the It Is Written Telecast.

Finley's meetings led to baptism decisions by nearly 3,200 new converts—more than on the day of Pentecost in Acts 2. Mark Finley tells the story of this modern miracle in a 1992 book entitled *The Cross and the Kremlin.*[1]

For decades Communism had attempted to stamp out Christianity in the Soviet Union. During Stalin's era an estimated 40,000 priests were murdered. Ninety-eight of every 100 orthodox churches were closed. Out of 179 Adventist pastors sent into exile in 1929, only four returned.

Christians of all faiths were imprisoned, tortured, and sent to concentration camps. Cautious historians estimate the death toll in the camps at ten to twenty million. One estimate puts the figure at closer to sixty to seventy million.

August of 1991

About 630 B.C., God told the prophet Habakkuk, "Look at the nations and watch—and be utterly amazed. For I am going to do something in your days that you would not believe, even if you were told" (Habakkuk 1:5).

Current events have again fulfilled that prophecy!

On August 20, 1991, for example, Communist tanks rumbled toward the Russian White House where Boris Yeltsin had barricaded himself with his officials. An attack seemed imminent.

Then the impossible happened. The commander of the Alpha Unit sent to attack refused orders. A furious KGB chief had to prepare another unit. But one by one, the commanders of nearly twenty units refused to attack—even under the threat of a firing squad.

Some 20,000 Soviet citizens, with a "whatever it takes" spirit, had spent the night outside the Russian White House. One of those 20,000 was a fourteen-year-old girl. She had cooked for the Yeltsin forces, ferrying hot soup from her home to the defenders.

At one point, as she sat on a steel barricade between Yeltsin's White House and the approaching Communist tanks, someone handed her a Bible. As she read, the peace of Christ flooded her heart (Mark Finley, *The Cross and the Kremlin*, pp. 14, 15).

The intended coup failed, and a nation of 280 million people now has religious and political freedom for the first time in ten centuries. During 1992, the Seventh-day Adventist Church conducted scores of major gospel crusades.

One of those crusades was held in Gorki, a city of more than two million people. For fifty years Communists used Gorki as an experimental center to try to blot out the name of God. The crusade ended with 1,700 people baptized on June 6 in what the August 20, 1992 *Adventist Review* called "possibly the largest baptism the country has seen in a thousand years." On the following two Sabbaths, 800 more people in Gorki were baptized into the Seventh-day Adventist Church.

More Berlin Walls

In the Introduction, I mentioned the book *Transforming Your Prayer Life*, by Pastor Bob Beltz, founder of the Cherry Hills Community Church in Denver, Colorado. In it, he discusses praying for specific countries.

On pages 88 and 89 of his book he directs attention to Matthew 24 and the return of Jesus. He decided, he said, to pray for several countries in which he had a special interest. One of those was Germany, a country he starting praying for in April of 1989.

In further comment, he added:

> "I have to admit that I certainly don't understand exactly how prayer works. God chooses, at times, to do amazing things based on the prayers of a single man or woman. At other times, there appears to be some sort of critical mass of prayer before God acts" (p. 90).

He wondered if, when he started praying in 1989, God needed just one more praying person to reach that critical mass.

"Who knows? But this we do know. There are
multitudes of Berlin Walls in the world today
needing the prayers of God's people to help
knock them down" (*Ibid.*).

Like Pastor Beltz, I don't understand just what it takes
for intercessory prayer to bring down Berlin Walls. But I
would like to suggest that we should especially pray for
these three countries: Cuba, Mainland China, and North
Korea.

Cuba: fervent prayers needed

I include Cuba because of a book I am just finishing: *I
Will Die Free.* This book tells the story of a young Seventh-
day Adventist pastor in Cuba, Noble Alexander, who was
arrested in 1962. He spent twenty-two years in Cuban
prisons, where inmates of all faiths were persecuted by
guards determined to eliminate Christianity in Cuba.

The cruelties inflicted were unbelievably horrible. Pastor
Alexander had been arrested as he arrived home from
conducting a revival meeting for Adventist youth. Not long
after his arrest, four guards attempted to break his spirit.
They took him to a dock next to a lake and tied his hands
and feet. They tied a rope around his waist, and repeatedly
threw him into the lake. Each time they would draw him
out just as he quit struggling.

Prisoners were kept in filthy cells without toilet facilities.
They were brought rotten food that smelled worse than the
human waste in the cells. All kinds of barbaric tortures
were inflicted. Many Christians perished rather than deny
Christ.

At the time of this writing, Castro's economy is in ruins.
He no longer gets support from the former Soviet Union.
In an attempt to win favor with Western countries, he
apparently has lessened his attempts to "re-educate" Cu-
bans. Let's pray that God will do whatever it takes to open
up Cuba for the gospel to again be proclaimed without
interference from the government.

Western Europe as a Berlin Wall

In many parts of Western Europe, less than ten percent of the people attend church. The March, 1990 issue of *Signs of the Times* reported that in the past twenty years the churches of Britain have lost over two million members and 5,000 clergy, and have closed 2,000 church buildings (p. 11). Weekly church attendance in England ranges from three to five percent of the population (*Ibid.*, p. 8).

In England, the Church of England had a twenty-four percent membership decline between 1970 and 1989, the Methodists twenty-six percent, the Presbyterian Church twenty-five percent, the Roman Catholic Church twenty-one percent, and the Baptists eighteen percent.

The author of the *Signs* article, David Marshall, edits *Family Life*—a Protestant journal published in England. He points out that the few denominations which are growing are largely the non-traditional ones, including Pentecostals and Seventh-day Adventists. The churches in decline, he says, are those which have refused to change. He feels that ancient liturgies and services which permit no congregational involvement need to go (*Ibid.*, p. 11).

Marshall suggests that the God the majority of Britons have rejected is a God who has never existed, and adds, "Growth groups like Seventh-day Adventists and John Stott's Evangelicals do not preach the non-biblical idea of an ever-burning hell, but present death as a sleep from which the dead awaken at the second coming. They present God as the Christ who stretched out His hands on the cross calling all men to know freedom from guilt, new life, and the assurance of salvation" (*Ibid.*).

North America as a Berlin Wall

What about North America? Polls indicate that about forty-four percent of Americans have no connection with any church. Many whose names are on the books seldom if ever attend.

How has it been in the Seventh-day Adventist churches of North America? Writing in *Celebration* magazine, Ron Watts notes that during the 1960s, a number greater than 100 percent of Adventist adult membership attended Sabbath School. Today that number is about forty-eight percent of the adult membership.

The August 17, 1992 issue of the *Pacific Union Recorder* estimated that between 500,000 and one million Seventh-day Adventists who are young adults in North America no longer attend church.

What will it take to bring them back?

Intensely interesting church services would no doubt help many of these half million non-attenders to come back. To my fellow pastors I would suggest: all of us need to do a better job of presenting messages that are strongly Scriptural, intensely interesting, and practical. And let's seek to present our messages with a deep conviction that is made effective by the presence of God's Spirit.

Perhaps church boards could also discuss what the author of the *Signs* article quoted earlier said about the churches of England: *Those that are growing are those that are not afraid of change.* While he mentioned Seventh-day Adventists as a church that is growing in England, change comes slowly.

There probably isn't an Adventist congregation in England or anywhere else that doesn't have members staunchly opposed to any kind of change. This attitude hinders the development of church services that have the power to get and hold attention.

If a Scriptural principle doesn't forbid doing some things differently, why not at least do a little experimentation? At both of my churches, for example, we have added ten minutes of singing between Sabbath School and the church service.

Many have appreciated this "something new." It reduces talking in the sanctuary and enhances a spirit of worship.

Pray. Pray. Pray. Pray.

To all my fellow believers, I would add: A revitalized church comes from revitalized and earnestly praying members. One time a Christian leader, taking a cue from Acts 1, suggested that we begin with this: "Pray. Pray. Pray. Pray."

Retired believers could do much through praying for renewal. Luke tells of Anna, a widow of eighty-five years, who "served God with fastings and prayers night and day" (Luke 2:37, KJV).

But we also need leaders who will pray, pray, pray, and pray. We need young people who will schedule daily times for earnest prayer. We need believers of all ages who will pray, pray, pray, and pray.

Let's not pray just for our own congregation. Each day's reading in George Knowles' *A World to Love*—a 1991 morning watch book—suggested a specific region or people group for which to pray on that day. This needs to become an ongoing prayer ministry.

The leadership at one evangelical congregation has organized "international prayer assignments" this way: the pastor suggested that each member ask the Holy Spirit to guide in deciding a nation for which to pray. Then at family prayer times, each participant prays for the nation he or she has selected. Some have even visited the land for which they are praying. Others write to a missionary in that country.

A spirit of supplication

God promised His ancient people that as they looked upon "the One they have pierced," He would pour out "a spirit of grace and supplication" (Zechariah 12:10).

That promise is still valid. Jesus said, "I, when I am lifted up from the earth, will draw all men to myself" (John 12:32). When we fall upon the Rock, Jesus said, our hearts are broken (Matthew 21:44). That brokenness, that sorrow for sin, is almost always accompanied by a spirit of humble supplication.

The following paragraph, penned in 1909, anticipates what the church can expect when it again develops a spirit of supplication:

> "A spirit of intercession was seen, even as was manifested before the great Day of Pentecost. Hundreds and thousands were seen visiting families and opening before them the word of God. Hearts were convicted by the power of the Holy Spirit, and a spirit of genuine conversion was manifest. On every side doors were thrown open to the proclamation of the truth" (*Testimonies for the Church*, vol. 9, p. 126).

Note two things: "a spirit of intercession" and "doors thrown open." I see the doors thrown open in the former Soviet Union as a promise of even more striking providences in the days ahead.

Let's seek the Lord in an unprecedented spirit of intercession! And with a "whatever it takes" spirit!

Promises of rain

In Palestine there are two rainy seasons. During Bible times, an early rain at planting time sprouted the seed and gave the crops a good start. A latter rain at harvest time filled out the grain.

In his Acts 2 sermon, Peter referred to the outpouring of the Holy Spirit on the day of Pentecost as a fulfillment of the prophecies of Joel 2 (Acts 2:16-21). That sermon led to the baptism of 3,000 people. Acts 2 ends with this

A spirit of intercession was seen, as before the great Day of Pentecost. A spirit of genuine conversion was seen.

summary statement about the growth that followed: "And

the Lord added to the church daily such as should be saved" (Acts 2:47, KJV).

The deep moving of the Holy Spirit at that time has been called "the early rain." These showers helped give the gospel a good start.

The "latter rain" can be expected just before Jesus returns. The following prophecy will again be fulfilled with even greater power:

> "And afterward I will pour out my Spirit on all people. Your sons and daughters will prophesy, your old men will dream dreams, your young men will see visions. Even on my servants, both men and women, I will pour out my Spirit in those days" (Joel 2:28, 29).

In this context, Joel mentions signs of the last days: blood, fire, and columns of smoke. He then gives this gracious promise:

"And it shall come to pass that all who call upon the name of the Lord shall be delivered" (Joel 2:32, RSV).

At that time conversions will take place with a rapidity similar to what happened in the opening chapters of Acts. Thousands will accept the gospel. Many of these new believers will almost immediately go to work sharing what they have discovered.

People on their knees

The launching of the gospel started with a group of people on their knees. "They joined together constantly in prayer" (Acts 1:14)—but they did more than pray. In a chapter entitled "Pentecost," the author of *The Acts of the Apostles* sums up what else they did:

■ Engaged in deep searching of hearts.

■ Humbled their hearts in true repentance.

■ Confessed their unbelief.

■ Put away their differences and drew close together in Christian fellowship.

■ Drew nearer and still nearer to God.

■ Developed an earnest desire to see lost people brought to Christ.

Note the last development listed. As their love for Christ grew, *they started really caring for people.* They wanted to get out and make a difference! For this, they sought the energy and power available through the Holy Spirit.

The following suggestion was given about 1895:

> "The descent of the Holy Spirit upon the church
> is looked forward to as in the future; but it is the
> privilege of the church to have it now. Seek for
> it, pray for it, believe for it. We must have it,
> and Heaven is waiting to bestow it" (*Evangelism*,
> p. 701).

Seek for it, pray for it, believe for it.

Christianity needs leaders who will seek and pray and believe. It needs hundreds of thousands of youth and young adults who will seek and pray and believe. God needs millions of all ages who will develop a spirit of supplication.

Usable ideas

1. Let's praise God for the work of God's Spirit in the former Soviet Union. Then let's ask Him to do whatever it takes to bring about similar developments in Cuba, Communist China, North Korea, and every other region where Communism still attempts to exclude Christianity. Pray also for God to do whatever it takes to awaken a sense of need in Western countries. Pray especially for your age group in your country.

2. As a family, you could develop an "international prayer ministry" in which each member selects a country for which to pray. Each could be alert for news items about

that country and share them at family prayer time. A specific country could be mentioned at meals by the one saying grace. Throughout the day, simple two-second "whatever it takes" prayers could be sent heavenward.

3. At the time of this writing, plans are in process for Seventh-day Adventist leadership to conduct 241 evangelistic campaigns in the former Soviet Union during 1993—the year of this book's first publication. Half of these crusades are to be conducted by national pastors and half by speakers from other countries. The largest is scheduled for mid-year by *It Is Written's* Mark Finley in Moscow's 35,000-seat Olympic Stadium.

During 1991 and 1992, Seventh-day Adventist membership in the Russian Republic has increased nearly 400 percent, from 6,700 to 26,000. Sixty-two new congregations have been formed, for a total of 192.[2] In the entire former Soviet Union, membership increased from 35,000 to 70,000.

As families, let's pray that in the years ahead an even greater growth will take place in the Russian Republic and in all the other Republics in that vast land of the former Soviet Union.

4. As a family, read and discuss the following two chapters in the book *The Acts of the Apostles:* "Pentecost" and "The Gift of the Spirit." Discuss what it means to "seek for, pray for, and believe for" the Holy Spirit.

Notes

1. *The Cross and the Kremlin* is available from Adventist Book Centers, or from Hart Research Center, P.O. Box 2377, Fallbrook, CA 92028.

2. Robert S. Folkenberg, *From the G.C. President* newsletter, Nov. 23, 1992.

CHAPTER EIGHT

Whatever It Takes and the Lord's Prayer

Do you ever think of the Lord's Prayer as a powerful and life-changing prayer of intercession?

I used to pray the Lord's Prayer only as a memorized formality—generally in a group setting. It had little significance in my devotional life. I never used it as an intercessory prayer.

That has changed. In this chapter I'd like to explain why I now pray it thankfully—even eagerly.

First, a few conclusions about the Lord's Prayer:

1. I see it as a pattern—not a memorized form.

Some think that the Lord's Prayer should be prayed in a set, liturgical way. I see it only as a pattern. When I pray it privately, I feel free to add other biblical expressions and words of my own.

2. I like the completeness of the Lord's Prayer.

It covers every possible need of the body of Christ and of individual members. The first three petitions are what some call "kingdom" requests:

- That God's name be hallowed

- That His kingdom come

- That His will be done

These petitions are for spiritual blessings that I, my family, and my church members need every day! And as I pray for the world-wide work of the church, what more could I ask?

Another three petitions concern personal needs:

- Daily bread

- Forgiveness

- Deliverance from temptation and from evil

These cover our need for food and other physical necessities, for the peace of mind that comes from being forgiven, and for protection in our walk with Christ.

3. I also like its simplicity.

Its wording is so simple that a child can understand it, yet it has a depth of meaning that challenges the wisest.

4. Lastly, I appreciate its brevity.

It illustrates what Jesus said in the Sermon on the Mount the first time He gave the Lord's Prayer: "When you pray, do not keep on babbling like pagans, for they think they will be heard because of their many words. Do not be like them" (Matthew 6:7, 8).

Adaptations I have made

When I use the Lord's Prayer privately, I often include other Bible verses. A favorite is this expression of adoration from a prayer of David: "Yours, O Lord, is the greatness and the power and the glory and the majesty and the splendor" (1 Chronicles 29:11).

Greatness! Power! Glory! Majesty! Splendor!

I see these as reminders that we serve an awesome God! Sometimes I cite David's words of adoration before each of the six petitions in the Lord's Prayer. I use them as "arguments" that invite God to act, as in this example: "Yours is the kingdom and the power and the glory and the majesty and the splendor, *therefore* hallowed be Thy name."

I also like to include a "whatever it takes" when I pray the Lord's Prayer: "Do *whatever it takes* to hallow your name in my own life, and in the lives of all the members in my congregations."

A depth of meaning not perceived

As we noted in chapter 5, Christ gave the Lord's Prayer two times—once in Matthew 6 and about a year later in Luke 11. It's in Luke 11 that the disciples requested, "Lord, teach us to pray" (Luke 11:1).

The book *Thoughts from the Mount of Blessing* gives this explanation:

> "Jesus gives them no new form of prayer. That which he has before taught them He repeats, as if He would say, You need to understand what I have already given. It has a depth of meaning you have not yet fathomed" (p. 103).

A depth of meaning not yet fathomed.

The *Mount of Blessing* chapter entitled "The Lord's Prayer" contains many helpful insights. Twice, for example, it connects the Lord's Prayer with the right-eousness of Christ.

We can hallow God's name, the author suggests, only through "the acceptance of the grace and righteousness of Christ" (p. 107). Forgiveness is a gift—a gift that can be ours because of "the spotless righteousness of Christ" (p. 116).

That understanding helps make the Lord's Prayer even more powerful! It is the fragrance of the righteousness of Christ that makes it life-changing. I do not come to God in my own goodness. I must always pray the Lord's Prayer trusting wholly in the merits of Christ.

Another helpful book

I have already mentioned the book *Transforming Your Prayer Life*. In it, Pastor Bob Beltz explains how he has used the Lord's Prayer to help him develop a strategy for a more effective prayer life. In his opening chapter, he speaks of his embarrassment when someone would inquire about his spiritual life. "It's going great," he would reply, "*but* I really need to work on my prayer life."

He now uses a strategy built around the Lord's Prayer. He sees seven components in this prayer and uses them as a pattern. In his book, he devotes a chapter to each of these seven parts.

He sees the first component as "Our Father," and titles it "Entering His Presence." As he enters God's presence to pray, he acknowledges his inability to pray. He says that he sometimes begins like this:

> "Father, I would like to spend some time today with You in prayer. You know that I don't know how to pray or have the ability to pray in a way that is pleasing to You and significant for me. Therefore I ask the Holy Spirit to help me pray as Your Word promises that He will" (p. 31).

He refers the reader to Romans 8:26, 27, where Paul assures us of the Spirit's help in our praying. Writes Pastor Beltz:

> "I get very specific about my need for help. If I want to have an hour of prayer, I ask the Holy Spirit to help me pray for an hour. If I know I don't have an hour, I ask for as long a period of prayer as I have time for" (*Ibid.*).

He may then ask the Spirit to make that time fruitful and enjoyable. His example has helped me start a new habit: that of praying about my praying.

Praying during morning walks

Here's how I am currently increasing the amount of time I actually pray during my morning devotions: After my study and journaling, I sometimes go outdoors and pray while walking one or two miles.

This morning I walked east just as the sun was rising. The sun turned my thoughts to Christ as the Sun of Righteousness. I keenly felt my dependence on the righteousness of Christ. With that sense of dependence, I prayed the Lord's Prayer on behalf of several groups: my immediate family, my two congregations, and Christians in Berrien County.

As I prayed, I also mentioned the work of God in specific parts of the world—especially in the former Soviet Union.

So many things in a garden invite prayer that I am also developing the habit of praying the Lord's Prayer while working in our yard and garden.

Let's take a brief look at the specific components in that prayer:

"Our Father"

I love the word *Our*. First, it takes in my immediate family. I see it as also including everyone in both my congregations. I sometimes broaden it to include every believer in my state or in North America.

I next linger on the word *Father*. This testimony of a father that I found in an old *Review* helps me better picture what God is like as my Father:

> "I stopped to look into the face of my sleeping
> son the other night. I had come home after a
> late appointment and had missed that last-mo-
> ment-before-sleep experience we usually share to-
> gether with God. I was deeply impressed that I
> need to look into this quiet face more often, less
> hastily, and realize the prize placed in my
> clumsy hands by an infinitely tender and patient

Creator. For fourteen years this boy has been entrusted to his mother and me.

"Next I moved to another room where lay in guileless sleep my lovely little daughter, a full-of-life ten. Morning and evening we worship together as a family, yet those last few prayer and tuck-in moments are the 'whipped-cream,' the 'topping' to her day. And nearly always she clings to me 'longer than I have time.'" (*Review and Herald*, February 26, 1959.)

As I pastor, I often feel like Solomon when he told the Lord, "I am only a little child and do not know how to carry out my duties" (1 Kings 3:7). The above story has helped me realize that in my dependence and need I, too, can throw my arms about my Father and cling to Him.

"Which art in heaven"

I see the *which art in heaven* as adoration. The One we call Father "created the heavens" (Isaiah 45:18). "He sits enthroned above the circle of the earth. . . . He stretches out the heavens like a canopy and spreads them out like a tent to live in" (Isaiah 40:22).

When I begin a prayer with "which art in heaven," it takes my thoughts out to the "heaven of heavens" (1 Kings 8:27, KJV). It reminds me of God's greatness and power. I see Him surrounded with "ten thousand times ten thousand, and thousands of thousands" of angels (Revelation 5:11). I see these powerful beings ready, at God's bidding, to come to the help of His children. The "which art in heaven" sets a mood of adoration and faith which can then pervade the rest of my prayer time.

"Hallowed be Thy name"

In *Transforming Your Prayer Life*, Pastor Beltz mentioned something that I have incorporated into my use of the Lord's Prayer. He points out that in the Old Testament, God revealed some things about Himself by compounding the name YHWH, or Jehovah, with words such as right-eousness, shepherding, and so on.

Thus, as we reach out in faith, God can become Jehovah our Righteousness (Jeremiah 23:6), Jehovah our Sanctifica-tion (Leviticus 20:7, 8), Jehovah our Shepherd (Psalm 23:1), Jehovah our Provider (Genesis 22:14), Jehovah our Healer (Exodus 15:26), Jehovah our Banner (Exodus 17:15), and Jehovah our Peace (Judges 6:24).

Since reading *Transforming Your Prayer Life*, I especially enjoy praying, "Hallowed be Thy name." In that part of my prayer I claim God as my personal Righteousness, as my Sanctification, and as my Shepherd. I look to Him as my Provider, my Healer, my Banner, and my Peace.

Then I often do the same on behalf of other individuals or groups on my prayer list for that day.

"Thy kingdom come"

This part of the Lord's Prayer adds delight for two reasons. First, it anticipates the return of Christ—an expec-tation heightened by the fast pace of events that began with the fall of the Berlin Wall in 1989.

But I find a second reason for delight in this petition. As I ask God to bring the kingdom of grace into the lives of those for whom I am praying, I can expect to see decided changes take place.

"Thy will be done"

S.D. Gordon calls this the greatest petition one can offer. "Every true prayer," he says, "comes under those four words."

This petition has become my favorite. Here's why: I have come to equate the will of God as synonymous with happiness.

I struggle with self-will, but those struggles are made easier by this realization: *God's will is synonymous with the greatest possible happiness a human being can enjoy.*

That gives me courage as I pray for family and friends and as I minister to and pray for my congregations. When, on someone's behalf, I ask God that His will be done, I am asking the greatest possible happiness for that person.

Asking for daily bread

In the Sermon on the Mount, Christ talked about our need for food, for clothing, and for similar physical necessities. He pointed to God's provision for the fowls of the air (Matthew 6:26, 27). He spoke of the beauty He gives to the flowers of the field (Matthew 6:28-30). "Don't worry about food or clothing," He said, adding this assurance,

---

God's will is synonymous with the greatest possible happiness that a human being can know.

"Seek first his kingdom and his righteousness, and all these things will be given to you as well" (Matthew 6:33).

A forgiving spirit

God helps "new creation" people (2 Corinthians 5:17) develop tender and forgiving spirits. We can then gladly pray, "Forgive us our sins, for we also forgive everyone who sins against us" (Luke 11:4).

Probably nothing does more to hinder our prayers than the resentments that we sometimes nurse. In this petition, I like to reword it: "Help us to put away all resentments and be forgiving so you can also forgive us."

Deliverance from evil

We are harassed by two foes: temptations from within and Satan from without. This final petition of the Lord's Prayer asks for deliverance from both: "And lead us not into temptation, but deliver us from the evil one" (Matthew 6:13).

Of the first, James wrote:

"When tempted, no one should say, 'God is
tempting me.' For God cannot be tempted by
evil, nor does He tempt anyone; but each is
tempted when, by his own evil desire he is
dragged away and enticed" (James 1:13, 14).

When an evil desire from within tempts me, I can *choose*
not to welcome that desire. As I back my decision with
prayer, God helps me not to think about the forbidden
subject.

When temptations come from without, I flee to God.
Isaiah 41:10-14 is my favorite passage for such situations.
In it, God tells me not to fear, adding "I will help you." He
says this *three times* in this passage!

And for both evils, God promises, "I will not allow you
to be tempted above what you are able, but with the
temptation will also make a way of escape." See 1 Corinthians 10:13.

Concluding with adoration

Webster suggests that to *adore* means (1) to worship or
honor, (2) to regard with reverent admiration and devotion,
or (3) to be extremely fond of. All three meanings describe
how I feel about God: I worship Him, I admire Him, and
I have every reason to be extremely fond of Him.

Matthew's version of the Lord's Prayer concludes with
adoration: "For thine is the kingdom, and the power, and
the glory, for ever" (Matthew 6:13, KJV).

If you are praying the Lord's Prayer privately, linger with
this concluding affirmation. Visualize God's kingdom.
Think of the Milky Way, and remember that there are
hundreds of billions of these star cities in God's kingdom.

Then think of the kind of power described in Psalm
33:6-9, where God simply speaks, and worlds appear.
Think, also, of God's recreative power—and His ability to
give you and those for whom you pray "a new heart"
(Ezekiel 36:26, 27).

Lastly, picture His glory—the glory of the self-sacrificing love described in John 1:14. See also the glory that will surround Christ at His second coming (Matthew 16:27).

A steadily increasing expectation

During the last few months, I have prayed the Lord's Prayer during my morning devotions and at additional times during the day. God's miracles of grace have steadily increased my faith—and have made me even more eager to keep praying the Lord's Prayer.

May I make these suggestions?

1. Become familiar with the ideas in this chapter. Then try spending five or ten minutes praying through the Lord's Prayer. Talk to God about each of the components.

2. Begin to think of the Lord's Prayer as an intercessory prayer. Pray it on behalf of individuals who need to be brought to Christ or who need a renewed experience with Him.

3. Try using portions of the Lord's Prayer as you come and go. I sometimes pray no more than this: "Our Father which art in heaven, do whatever it takes to hallow Your name."

You can send that kind of abbreviated petition heavenward many times during a day as you are walking, driving, and so on. In praying this way, I often recall the suggestion in a previous chapter that when I come to God as His child, my requests "are music in His ears."

4. For additional insights, check a Christian book store for either or both of the books mentioned: *Thoughts from the Mount of Blessing* and *Transforming Your Prayer Life*.

CHAPTER NINE

Why Prayer Changes Things

S atan dreads nothing but prayer," Samuel Chadwick once said.

"The one concern of the devil is to keep the saints from praying," he added. "He fears nothing from prayerless studies, prayerless work, prayerless religion. He laughs at our toil, mocks at our wisdom, but trembles when we pray."

Is the preceding true? And if so, why?

In Luke 11, Jesus said: "Ask, and it will be given to you; seek and you will find; knock and the door will be opened to you" (Luke 11:9). The implication is that if you don't ask, you are going to miss out on a lot of good things.

We discuss Luke 11:9 in my Workshop in Prayer class, and one time a student commented, "When we finally get to heaven and see all the good things we didn't get because we didn't ask, we will wish we had done more asking!"

James wrote to certain believers: "You have not, because you ask not" (James 4:2).

Apparently it is God's plan to grant us, in answer to the prayer
of faith, blessings that He otherwise would not be able to give.

Reasoning out the above conclusion

The logic behind the preceding conclusion is this: We
are involved in a "great controversy" between God and
Satan. (A later chapter takes a look at Revelation 12:7-9,
Isaiah 14:12-14, and Ezekiel 28:12-19—scriptures that give
the background for this conflict). Apparently there are
ground rules in this battle that neither side can violate.

For example, Satan has only limited power over the
human race. He can't pick you up and drop you into the
middle of an ocean. And while he can tempt you, he can't
force you to sin.

God, likewise, operates under certain "battlefield restrictions"—restraints imposed by His own character. He will
never use flattery or deceit. He never resorts to force to

"Satan cannot endure to have his powerful rival appealed to, for he fears and trembles before His strength
and majesty. At the sound of fervent prayer, Satan's
whole host trembles" (*Testimonies*, vol. 1, p. 346).

---

keep you from entering into temptation. And because
temptation develops character, He does not provide a
temptation-free environment.

Suppose you pray for a tempted child—your own or a
younger brother or sister or friend. Could it be that your
prayer gives God the right to do more for that person than
He otherwise would be able to do?

Satan schemes to hinder everything God wants to do
for the tempted one. And until your ask, God appears to
be somewhat limited in how much He can do without
protests from Satan. If God works with extra power, Satan
can object, "God, you have no right to do so much for this
individual."

But when you ask for that extra help, God can tell Satan, "I have been invited to do this."

Let me say it again: *I believe that Christ's invitation to ask implies that it is part of God's plan to grant us, in answer to the prayer of faith, blessings that He otherwise would not be able to give without Satan running interference.*

And why does Satan tremble when we earnestly ask God for help? Because he knows the power and majesty of Christ. He trembles when we appeal to our powerful Advocate.

Satan despises the will of God. But he also fears it. And, as S.D. Gordon says in his book *Quiet Talks on Prayer*, "the purpose of prayer is to get God's will done."[1]

Fear of Christ's power and majesty and fear of God's will—these, I believe, are why Satan trembles when you sincerely pray.

Prayer and church growth

During a recent board meeting at my Coloma congregation, an elder commented: "We've got to encourage our people to pray. Only a praying church grows."

Is he right?

The book of Acts started with 120 believers spending ten days in heart-searching, repentance, confession, and prayer.

The results? Within a year's time, that group of 120 had become tens of thousands.

The first seven chapters of Acts span about a year. After Christ ascended to Heaven, the disciples and other believers "all joined together constantly in prayer" (Acts 1:14). After they had spent ten days in prayer and in drawing close to the Lord and to each other, God gave the Holy Spirit. Peter's Acts 2 sermon led to the baptism of 3,000 people.

That was just the beginning! By Acts 4, the Jerusalem congregation had increased to 5,000 men (Acts 4:4). Add the women and youth, and they probably numbered at least 15,000 believers.

Acts 5 records continued growth—with "multitudes of both men and women" added to the church (Acts 5:14, KJV). And Acts 6 says: "The number of disciples in Jerusalem increased rapidly, and a large number of priests became obedient to the faith" (Acts 6:7).

We don't know how many Christians there were in Jerusalem at the end of that first year. In his *Basic New Testament Evangelism*, Faris Whitesell writes: "The membership of the Jerusalem church at this point has been estimated as anywhere from 25,000 to 100,000" (p. 137).[2]

That would be quite a congregation! And it grew to that number in about a year!

Acts 8-12 covers the next dozen years and tells of the expansion of the gospel into Palestine and Syria—with spectacular growth in those regions (Acts 9:31, 42; 11:21, 24; 12:24).

Chapters 13-28 cover another fifteen years and tell about the spread of Christianity throughout Asia Minor—again with remarkable growth (Acts 13:49; 14:1; 16:5; 17:2; 18:8).

As Luke tells this story of early church growth, what one topic do you think he mentions more often than any other?

Not organization. Not well-laid plans. Not witnessing. *But prayer.*

Prayer in early Adventist history

As I prepared a *Faith and Prayer* syllabus for my "Workshop in Prayer" classes at Andrews University, I discovered some interesting things about prayer in the early history of the Seventh-day Adventist Church. For people then, as now, prayer often got crowded out.

James and Ellen White and other leaders attempted to get people to pray more—but with limited success. In 1862, as the Civil War was raging, Ellen White repeatedly wrote about the power of prayer. In a message entitled "Philosophy and Vain Deceit" she warned that Satan was leading many to believe that prayer to God is useless. "It's just a form," some argued.

In an attempt to refute this notion, Ellen White pointed to Elijah and Daniel and commented, "Satan is enraged at the sound of fervent prayer, for he knows that he will suffer loss" (*Testimonies for the Church*, vol. 1, p. 295). She then added:

> "The prayer of faith is the great strength of the Christian and will assuredly prevail against Satan. That is why he insinuates that we have no need of prayer. The name of Jesus, our Advocate, he detests; and when we earnestly come to Him for help, Satan's host is alarmed. It serves his purpose well if we neglect the exercise of prayer" (*Ibid,* p. 296).

Later that year, in a message entitled "The Power of Satan," attention was directed to Christ as "the mighty Conqueror." In that context, Ellen White suggested that Satan well knows the power believers can have over him when their strength is in Christ. "When they humbly entreat the mighty Conqueror for help," she added, "the weakest believer in the truth, relying firmly upon Christ, can successfully repulse Satan and all his host" (*Ibid.,* p. 340).

The concluding paragraphs suggest:

> "Satan cannot endure to have his powerful rival appealed to, for he fears and trembles before His strength and majesty. At the sound of fervent prayer Satan's whole host trembles" (*Ibid.,* p. 346).

Fasting and praying about the Civil War

That was in 1862. Early in 1865, Adventists, like other Americans, had become very weary of the Civil War. Adventists were especially concerned about the South. They longed for an opportunity to take the gospel to the slaves.

Through General Conference Committee action, James White and other leaders asked Adventists to fast and pray for four days, from Wednesday, March 1, till the close of the following Sabbath. These assemblies for confession of sin and urgent prayer took place at 1:00 p.m. daily and twice on Sabbath.

Within an impressively short time, the North won and Lee surrendered at Appomattox. Adventists saw it as an answer to prayer. (For confirmation of this illustration, see Mervyn Maxwell's academy text *Moving Out*, pp. 127, 128.)

But once the war ended, the spirit of prayer got crowded out again. In 1867 Ellen White wrote, "I inquire a hundred times a day, How can God prosper us? There is but little praying. In fact, prayer is almost obsolete" (*Ibid.*, p. 566).

Church administrators are so busy! Pastors are equally busy! Church members live busy, pressure-filled lives. Has prayer again become "almost obsolete"?

"The greatest victories"

In another crisis situation, Jacob found himself wrestling with an angel. As he prayed, he cried out, "I will not let you go unless you bless me" (Genesis 32:26).

From that experience, the author of *Patriarchs and Prophets* draws this lesson:

> "The greatest victories to the church of Christ or to the individual Christian are not those that are gained by talent or education, by wealth or by the favor of men. They are those victories that are gained in the audience chamber with God, when earnest, agonizing faith lays hold upon the mighty arm of power" (p. 203).

Talent. How often I have wished God had given me more talent. I would love, for example, to be able to carry a tune so I could lead rousing song services.

Education. Here at Andrews University, students often see grades as all-important. But top grades, even if one is going into medicine, are not where the greatest victories are gained.

Wealth. If the church had billions in resources, that probably would not greatly increase the number of people who are converted, unless we were also fervently praying.

The favor of men. Politicians seek it. Business executives seek it. Even church administrators would be delighted if the church had it.

None of these are the secret for success. *Both for the church and for the individual Christian, the real victories are gained in the audience chamber with God.*

Why, then, aren't we seeking God in prayer? How can we find time to pray? We'll take a look at that in the next chapter.

Notes

1. S.D. Gordon, *Quiet Talks on Prayer* (New York: Grosset & Dunlap, 1904), p. 177.

2. Faris Daniel Whitesell, *Basic New Testament Evangelism* (Grand Rapids, Mich.: Zondervan Publishing House, 1949), p. 137. Used by permission.

CHAPTER TEN

Finding Time to Pray —and to Listen

P rayer is the most important thing in my life," said Martin Luther. "If I should neglect prayer for a single day, I should lose a great deal of the fire of faith."

What's *your* top priority as you start a new day? Breakfast? Work? Getting to class? Or, if you have children, getting them off to school?

And to what do you give first priority in the evening? Homework? Television? Extra work from the office?

Do you also schedule some morning and evening time for God? And if you have a family, do you plan a time for fellowship and prayer with them?

In Psalm 5, sometimes called the "morning psalm," David wrote, "In the morning you hear my voice; in the morning I lay my requests before you" (Psalm 5:3).

His thoughts also went to God in the evening. In Psalm 4, the "evening psalm," he prays, "Let the light of your face shine upon us" (v. 6).

And in Psalm 63 he adds, "On my bed I remember you, I think of you during the night watches" (v. 6).

101

Are we enjoying similar experiences?

An unused key

Consider again this statement of Jesus: "Ask and it will be given to you; seek and you will find; knock and the door will be opened to you" (Luke 11:9).

Does this imply that asking, along with seeking and knocking, is sort of a key?

The little book *Steps to Christ* poses this question:

> "Why should the sons and daughters of God be reluctant to pray, when prayer is the key in the hand of faith to unlock Heaven's storehouse, where are treasured the boundless resources of Omnipotence?" (pp. 94, 95).

The boundless resources of omnipotence! But how can we draw on these resources if we neglect to use the key?

Imagine having a late-model car in your garage. But it never gets driven. You never have time to take the key out of the drawer where you keep it! The key never gets used.

Preposterous? I agree. But I must ask: Why do so many of us leave the key of faith and prayer in the drawer? One survey has indicated that the typical believer in America spends about three minutes a day in prayer.

Possible reasons include:

- Life's cares, pressures, and demands.

- Attempting to do too much.

- Watching TV so late we don't get up in time for devotional study and unrushed prayer.

- Not really believing that prayerless living accomplishes almost nothing for eternity.

Dependence on whom?

A mistake that I often make is trying to do too much. Do you ever have a similar problem?

At times, when Christ and the disciples ministered to people, so many were coming and going that "they did not even have a chance to eat." One one such occasion, Jesus suggested that He and the disciples take a break. "Come with me by yourselves," He said, "to a quiet place and get some rest" (Mark 6:31).

Christ is full of tenderness and compassion for all in His service. It's our duty to get adequate rest. Success comes, not from human effort alone, but from dependence upon God.

Shortly after I became a Christian, I read a biography of Christ called *The Desire of Ages*. In the chapter "Come Rest Awhile," the author suggests that while we are to labor earnestly for the lost, we must also take time for meditation, for prayer, and for the study of the Word of God. Then comes this sentence:

> "Only the work accomplished with much prayer, and sanctified by the merit of Christ, will in the end prove to have been efficient for good" (p. 362).

In John 15, Jesus is unmistakably clear about priorities. He is the Vine; we are the branches (John 15:1-6).

> "If a man remains in me and I in Him, he will bear much fruit; apart from me you can do nothing. If anyone does not remain in me he is like a branch that is thrown away and withers" (John 15:5, 6).

Apart from Me you can do nothing. Do we really believe that?

Of schedules and patterns

To have adequate time for prayer, I suggest two strategies:

1. Develop a schedule that allows time for unhurried prayer.

2. Select a pattern to follow when you pray.

First, a schedule. Paul probably wasn't thinking about a schedule for prayer when he wrote, "Everything should be done in a fitting and orderly way" (1 Corinthians 14:40). But the advice fits.

If you are a morning person, you could schedule devotional time for the early morning. If an evening person, schedule your devotional time for the evening, with a quick review the next morning. Or perhaps you could plan some devotional time during the lunch hour.

Two things help me stick to my schedule for devotional time: (1) getting to bed at a reasonable time, and (2) eating a light supper. An early, light supper increases the refreshment you get from your sleep. If you are of high school or college age, here's an important sentence from the book *Education:*

> "Since the work of building up the body takes place during the hours of rest, it is essential, especially in youth, that sleep should be regular and abundant" (p. 205).

A physician shared this with me: On days when he had obtained adequate sleep, he accomplished more in eight hours than he could in twelve hours when he didn't get sufficient sleep.

The same is true when we pray. "Prayer," says Taylor Bunch in *Prevailing Prayer*, "is the greatest of all timesavers. By making the work of the day go more smoothly and efficiently, the Lord can and does more than make up the time spent in prayer" (p. 47).

Next, a pattern. Currently, I use a pattern which includes the "something new" discoveries I wrote about in Chapter 4. For a journal, I prefer a 5-1/2 by 8-1/2 three-ring notebook with a supply of non-lined paper. I take a sheet and divide it into these three parts: "Yesterday," "Something new," and "Whatever it takes." This becomes my outline for journaling.

Yesterday

Under the heading "Yesterday," I write about the events of the previous twenty-four hours. For this aspect of journaling, I am indebted to Bill Hybels and the suggestions he makes in *Too Busy Not to Pray*. (He credits Gordon MacDonald and his book *Ordering Your Private World* for the "yesterday" idea.)

MacDonald suggests going to a drug store and buying a spiral notebook. Each new day, write "Yesterday" at the top of the page. Then briefly recount yesterday's events. Options include people you interacted with, decisions, mistakes, what you intended to accomplish but didn't, and so on.

"Examine yourselves," Paul suggests (2 Corinthians 13:5). MacDonald points out that most of us lead unexamined lives. We repeat the same mistakes day after day. Taking a few minutes for reflection about the previous day forces us to examine our lives and to deal with our sins and mistakes.

Under "Yesterday" I start by listing any providences or special blessings of the previous day. I generally conclude with mention of errors in judgment and specific sins that need to be dealt with. If I spoke irritably to my wife, I write that down and then ask God's forgiveness—and hers.

True confession is specific. When the Hebrews asked for a king, then repented, they were very specific: "We have added to all our other sins the evil of asking for a king" (1 Samuel 12:19).

This way of dealing with yesterday's sins helps keep them from being repeated. By the time I write down a half dozen times that "I sinned yesterday in becoming irritable," I get the point: It's time to stop!

Something new discoveries

When I finish "Yesterday," I go to God's Word. I then use about half of the back side of my sheet for my "something new" discoveries. If I find nothing new, I write out an appropriate verse I can include in that day's thoughts and prayers. For this I generally use about half of the back side of my sheet.

I shared some "something new each day" ideas on pages 54-57 in the chapter "Teach Us to Pray." Here are additional suggestions about how to discover new insights:

■ When you find a statement in which God speaks to you, examine the context. In Ephesians 5, for example, husbands are told, "Love your wives" (v. 25). If you are a husband, read the entire chapter. "How to" suggestions include: shun foolish talk (vv. 3-5), be Spirit-filled (v. 18), make melody in your heart and home by singing hymns (v. 19), give thanks for everything (v. 20).

■ Sometimes use a Bible with marginal references. When I look up two or three cross references and compare similar statements on the same subject, I almost always find a new insight.

■ At times, read from a version different from the one you normally use.

■ Read from a morning devotional book. In my Workshop in Prayer class, we use portions of *My Life Today*. The comments with the text cited for the day often suggest a new insight.

Whatever it takes requests

On the bottom half of the back side of my notebook page, I write my "Whatever it takes" requests for that day.

Generally I start with personal and family needs. The next are local ministry needs. The final requests usually have to do with the world-wide work of the church. With each request I generally jot down the reference to an appropriate Bible promise or Scripture.

Here are the requests I wrote down for today:

Personal and family needs

1. A keener awareness of Christ's presence (Matthew 28:19).

2. An overflowing gratitude for our family garden (Psalm 104:14).

3. To let my wife know how much I appreciate her (Ephesians 5:25).

Local ministry needs

4. Guidance for a church board that meets this evening to make some important decisions (Proverbs 3:5, 6).

World needs

5. The ministry of angels to new Christians in the former Soviet Union (Hebrews 1:14).

I like to begin by asking for specific blessings needed *this very day.* During my journaling tomorrow, I will record the extent to which today's requests have been granted.

"This very day" requests

If a plan like this appeals to you, I suggest starting with just two or three requests. One of these could be for a spiritual blessing that you can expect God to give that very day.

Here's a list, with accompanying references, of a few blessings for which I have recently prayed:

- An increased conviction of sin (John 16:7, 8).

- An affectionate longing for God (Psalm 42:1, 2).

- A greater trust in Christ's righteousness (Isaiah 64:6 and Jeremiah 23:6).

- A sense of the preciousness of Christ (Matthew 13:45, 46).

- To really enjoy God today (Zephaniah 3:17).

If I do my part and maintain a spirit of reaching out after God, I can expect these blessing *that very day.*

The first morning that I asked God to help me relax and really enjoy Him, I had read this:

> "The Lord your God is with you; he is mighty to save. He will take great delight in you, he will quiet you with his love, he will rejoice over you with singing" (Zephaniah 3:17).

He will rejoice over you with singing! That implies He wants us to also enjoy Him!

My wife and I have a couple of trellises by our house, where we often plant a blue variety of morning glory. In the early morning, the blossoms are fresh and beautiful. One morning as I stopped to think and pray near one of the trellises, I thought, "God is like these morning glory blossoms—He, too, has a glory that is fresh, clear, and beautiful. And unlike these blossoms, His glory doesn't fade."

All through August and September, the morning glory blossoms remind me to take "enjoyment of God" pauses.[1]

One cannot always be thinking about God. Many kinds of work—operating equipment, doing surgery, teaching a class—demand one's full attention. One can train the mind, however, to reach out to God whenever there is a pause. And even during the busiest moments, there can be a background awareness of God's presence.

Ministry requests

There is no pleasure that equals that of being a blessing to another person. That's a joy open to everyone!

I especially like to draw a request from this promise to Abraham: "I will bless you . . . and you will be a blessing" (Genesis 12:2). That's a promise for us too! God not only blesses—He also wants to make us a blessing.

When my wife and I travel, we usually take along several attractive books to share. (One favorite is *Happiness Digest.*) When appropriate, we like to give a copy to service station attendants, motel clerks, and others.

Sometimes we have an experience that really stands out. Last spring, for example, we pulled into a service station at a small town in Kansas. While I filled our tank, a van with six girls stopped on the other side of the same pump.

The driver was about seventeen. As I visited with her, I discovered that they were from a Davenport, Iowa, high school. It was the spring break. Along with an adult sponsor, they were on their way to Texas. We had taken several kinds of books, and the driver readily accepted a variety—one book for each of her passengers.

(If you aren't in the habit of taking attractive books to give away when you travel, here's a promise from Ecclesiastes 11:6 to consider: "Sow your seed in the morning, and at evening let not your hands be idle, for you do not know which will succeed, whether this or that, or whether both will do equally well.")

I didn't know if any of those high school students were Christians. But as we drove on I thanked God for the opportunity of giving them several books that could help awaken an interest in His Word. God had again fulfilled His Genesis 12:2 promise: "I will make you a blessing."

Another idea: Often one can be a blessing to someone just by making a phone call. Perhaps you can speak a word of encouragement to a person needing it. As I close a telephone visit with someone, if it seems appropriate, I may pray with that individual.

If you currently aren't getting a lot of answers to prayer, test Genesis 12:2. Expect God to make you a blessing to at least one person each day. As He does, keep a brief record of good experiences and special providences. Keeping God's blessings fresh in memory will strengthen your faith. It will motivate you to claim more and still more!

Time for listening, too

Have you ever conversed with someone who attempted to do all the talking?

We speak of prayer as conversation with a Friend. That needs to be two-way. In his book, *Yours for the Asking,* Edwin Gallagher writes: "Unless God speaks back to us in prayer, we are merely talking *to* God, not *with* Him, and that is not prayer" (p. 51).

Bill Hybels, in *Too Busy Not to Pray,* includes a chapter he calls "Importance of Listening." He suggests that it's ironic that "most of the time we think of prayer as talking to God, rarely stopping to wonder whether God might want to talk to us. But as I have studied prayer and prayed, I've sensed God saying, 'If we enjoy a relationship, why are you doing all the talking? Let me get a word in somewhere'" (pp. 107, 108).

I'm guilty too! When I pray, I've often done far more talking than listening. Gradually, I'm learning how to listen. I've never heard an audible voice, but God speaks very distinctly.

The first way God speaks is through His Word. That's why in my journaling, I almost always prayerfully read from God's Word before spending time in prayer.

During my prayer time, He also speaks through the impressions of the Holy Spirit. In *Too Busy Not to Pray*, Hybels makes a number of suggestions I find very helpful. In the chapter "How to Hear God's Leadings," he says that he regularly asks God, "What next?" His first question, he writes, is "What's the next step in developing my character?"

"I almost always hear from God when I ask that question," he adds, "because there's always an edge He is trying to knock off my life" (p. 121).

Think of questions you could ask, and give this a try. You won't hear an audible voice, but the Holy Spirit loves to answer. Sometimes He'll bring conviction about changes you may need to make. At other times He'll bring to mind passages that build faith.

Just do it

To develop new devotional habits, is there any better time to start than *now?*

About a month before the 1992 presidential election, the candidates were disputing about the conditions under which they would be willing to debate. The October 2, 1992 issue of the South Bend *Tribune* published an editorial entitled "Just Do It."

And, eventually, they did.

In his book *Transforming Your Prayer Life*, Bob Beltz included several pages that he entitled "Just Do It!" He told of a friend who had gone to the Cooper Clinic in Dallas,

Texas. Those at the clinic explained that to make exercise a habit, he needed to do it at least five times a week.

If our goal is only three times a week, the staff said, it's too easy to make excuses. At five times a week, exercising is much more likely to become a habit.

When I started journaling, I tried to do it seven days a week. My average now is five plus a weekend review. On Friday evening I like to review the something-new insights and answered prayers of the week, and write a condensed summary of that week's blessings and leadings.

Even when I don't journal, however, I make it a habit to spend some time in God's Word and in prayer.

To get started, the important thing for now is: *Just do it!*

Getting started

1. Think about your schedule. Where could you set aside a half hour for devotional study and prayer?

Your day may be so full that you will need a strong "whatever it takes" spirit to establish a quiet time. But test this thesis: *You'll accomplish more in eight hours after you spend a half hour in Bible study and prayer than you will in twelve hours without prayer.*

2. If you are open to some journaling during your quiet time, select a simple pattern and give it a try. For an easy beginning, jot down a verse or a "something new" discovery, and some brief reflections about the previous day.

3. If you haven't already done so, start a "whatever it takes" prayer list.

4. If you don't regularly take time to listen as you pray, give it a try. Ask some "What next?" questions.

For further ideas, check a Christian bookstore for a copy of Bill Hybel's *Too Busy Not to Pray.*

Notes

1. The front cover of a 1993 adult devotional book published by the Review and Herald Publishing Association pictures a morning glory blossom. This book, entitled *Morning Praise*, is by Bob and Marie Spangler.

CHAPTER ELEVEN

Questions and Concerns About Prayer

Picture yourself and Jesus as visiting together in your living room. He invites you to ask anything you want about prayer or about related concerns. What would you ask?

Here are some questions pastors get asked. With each, I will attempt to summarize possible answers.

1. "Where is God when someone you love gets killed in a car accident?"

Donna lived with our family for two years while attending Andrews University. Returning to her home state, she eventually met a young man who asked her to marry him. Then one evening she was killed by a drunk driver who ran a stop sign.

I called Donna's mother, a single parent, in an attempt to offer comfort. Donna was her only child. "I've not only lost Donna," she said, "but now I will never have any grandchildren."

"Why," she asked, "didn't God keep this from happening?"

What would you have told her?

We live in what Jeremiah called "the land of the enemy" (Jeremiah 31:16). Jesus told a parable in which someone sowed weeds in a wheat field (Matthew 13:24-30). "An enemy has done this," the owner told his servants.

But this we also know: "In all things God works for the good of those who love him" (Romans 8:28). When an unexpected tragedy comes, we too can say, "An enemy did this." And in the resurrection, the God of all comfort will make it right with us.

2. "Why does a God of love allow injustice and hate and war? How can He let little children starve to death?"

An understanding of "the great controversy" helps us know why God, for the sake of the entire universe, allows such things.

That controversy is much bigger than any earthly conflict. It started in heaven (Revelation 12:7-9). Isaiah 14:12-14 and Ezekiel 28:11-19 reveal the developments leading up to this conflict. An angel named Lucifer rebelled against the authority of God. That made it rebellion against God's will as expressed in His law.

In his declaration of war, Lucifer screamed, "I will . . . I will . . . I will . . . I will . . . I will" (Isaiah 14:12-14). He argued that he could do a better job of governing the universe than God.

Because of his high position and because he used flattery and deceit, Lucifer convinced one-third of the angels to join his rebellion (Revelation 12:4). Then Adam and Eve's sin got us involved.

For the future security of the universe, God has had to give Satan a chance to demonstrate whether or not the abolition of law would bring greater happiness.

Lucifer has been behind every war, every injustice. He has imparted his temperament to so many people that hate, crime, and murder are rampant.

Satan also knows enough about the secrets of nature to stir up storms and bring about famines through drought. God has allowed these disasters, but only within certain limits. He has told Satan, as He says to the waves of the ocean, "Thus far, and no further."

God could put such powerful chains on Satan that he could never cause another storm or war—and very shortly He will, as described in Revelation 20.

Meanwhile, it has been necessary to allow sin to demonstrate what lawlessness is like. Never again will anyone in the universe be deceived. "Trouble will not come a second time" (Nahum 1:9).

3. God already knows what I need. Why tell Him what He already knows?

It's true that God knows our every need. But it's also true that as human beings, we tend to become self-sufficient and proud. One reason God wants us to ask is that asking helps us remember our dependence upon Him.

4. How can I know if what I am asking God for is His will?

The first thing to check is this: What does the Bible say that might apply to this request? What Bible principles apply?

At times God also guides by providences—shut doors, open doors. These, however, should always be compared with Scripture.

Check, also, with godly friends. Get their thinking. If you are praying about a problem, try to find a solution-oriented friend to counsel with.

As you think and pray, be open to the leadings of the Holy Spirit. Seeks the Spirit's input by asking questions such as these: "Will what I'm asking bring honor to God? Is it in the best interest of my spouse, or my children? Might it come between me and God—or will it draw me closer to Him?"

5. If I'm pretty sure something is God's will, why keep on asking and asking? Shouldn't one request be sufficient?

Prayer does not change God—it changes us. We may need to search our hearts and repent of sin. As we keep bringing our requests, the Holy Spirit has opportunity to lead us to repentance.

On Mount Carmel, Elijah prayed for rain seven times before God answered. During those prayers he searched his heart for any evidence of pride or of sin. An Ellen White comment in volume 2 of the *SDA Bible Commentary* suggests this about Elijah's experience:

> "As he searched his heart, he seemed to be less and less, both in his own estimation and in the sight of God. It seemed to him that he was nothing, and that God was everything; and when he reached the point of renouncing self, while he clung to the Saviour as his only strength and righteousness, the answer came. The servant appeared, and said, 'Behold, there ariseth a little cloud out of the sea, like a man's hand'" (p. 1035).

"The chief purpose of prayer," someone has pointed out, "is to bring us into harmony with God." It may be that we will need to pray and examine our hearts over a period of time before our desires become one with God's desires and will.

6. I hear about people who pray for an hour or longer. How can anyone find something to say to God for that long?

Jesus sometimes even prayed all night (Luke 6:12). But I don't picture an hour-long prayer or an all-night prayer as nonstop talking.

If prayer is to be conversation, there's got to be time for listening. That can sometimes take the form of meditation. If you are in a lighted area, let God speak to you through His Word. You can then respond to what He says.

Consider these further suggestions when you want to pray for an hour or more:

■ Whenever possible, go to your prayer time rested. A refreshed, alert mind and body help keep prayer fervent.

■ At times, do some of your praying in the out-of-doors. Wildflowers in bloom, the song of a bird, the warmth of the spring sun—all can become invitations to pray a littler longer than usual. I like to pray while hiking—sometimes longer than usual—as I watch summer clouds move across the sky.

For a still different experience, take a Bible and sit under a tree or by a stream, read a bit, and then talk to God about what you have read.

■ Try praying through a Bible book, using a passage or chapter at a time. I recently started praying through the Psalms. I first read the psalm and write key ideas and/or my "something new" discovery on that day's journal page. With an open Bible, I then talk to God about the ideas. You can take a good ten or fifteen minutes just praying through Psalm 103, for example.

And the Psalms contain something for everybody!

> "There are psalms for every mood, for every need: psalms for the disappointed, for the discouraged, for the aged, for the despairing, for the sick, for the sinner; and psalms for the youthful, for the vigorous, for the hopeful, for the faithful, believing child of God, for the triumphant saint" (*SDA Bible Commentary*, vol. 3, p. 620).

7. How can busy moms and dads find time to pray alone with each other?

Try this: upon arising, kneel at your bedside with your arms about each other. Then pray for yourselves and for your children.

Remember also: the more you love Jesus and study His life, the more you will become like Him. That makes you a more wonderful person to know and love—and to pray for and with. Let that love be the force that draws you together for prayer.

As I was working on this chapter, my wife was out in the kitchen. As I paused there a few moments, she embraced me. I suggested a moment of prayer. We both prayed and gave thanks for our children.

Try something similar on occasion. Make it a habit, also, to express appreciation to each other. A chapter in *The Ministry of Healing* entitled "Builders of the Home" contains this suggestion:

> "Cultivate that which is noblest in yourselves, and be quick to recognize the good qualities in each other. The consciousness of being appreciated is a wonderful stimulus and satisfaction. Sympathy and respect encourage the striving after excellence, and love itself increases as it stimulates to nobler aims" (p. 361).

Try it! It really works!

8. How can parents help children develop good prayer habits?

Two things are important: your example, and starting early.

On occasion, help your little ones say a thank-you prayer before meals. Schedule a few minutes of unrushed time for family worship each evening, and assist the children in saying a simple prayer.

If you are a father, whenever possible tuck in and pray with your little ones at night. That custom provides an excellent opportunity to help your children each develop a prayer habit.

When he was teaching family life classes at Weimar College, Dick Winn told his students how he helped his preschool son and daughter to develop the habit of personal devotions. He recorded short worship stories or texts of Scripture on cassettes and encouraged them to turn on their own tape recorder and listen to it for private worship in their room. His instructions included a suggestion about prayer.

Winn did this in addition to regular family worship.

9. How does one keep family prayer and worship from becoming boring to the children?

Three principles help: (1) use interesting material adapted to the age of the children, (2) keep worship remarks and prayers brief, and (3) use lots of variety.

One time in a Ministry of Prayer class at the Andrews University Seminary, I asked students to share ideas about how to have variety in family worship. Suggestions they made included:

■ In families with small children, prepare a worship notebook as a Sabbath afternoon activity. Each page could have a given theme, with a song, a text, a picture, and a story or poem. Cover completed pages with plastic and then let children take turns choosing which page they want for evening worship.

■ With primary-age children, you could collect leaves and then press them. Use spray paint to transfer leaf images to the pages of a notebook. Write a Bible promise within each leaf image. Take turns letting each child choose a promise to pray about in the worship prayer. Take time, also, to teach them how to include a Bible verse as they pray. Coach them in actually doing so.

■ Occasionally conduct a thanksgiving service. Read a few verses from any of the last five Psalms, then invite each family member to mention something from that day for which he or she is thankful.

■ Use a modern-speech version and take several days or weeks to read a short Bible book or part of a gospel, by reading a few paragraphs at a time. Let all who are old enough participate in the reading by changing readers every paragraph or two. The one leading out could ask questions which spark discussion.

■ Develop a slide presentation to use occasionally. Slides could be from a family trip or other cherished family activity. My wife has developed slide presentations that illustrate each of the following hymns: "This Is My

Father's World," "How Great Thou Art," and "All Things Bright and Beautiful." Some good worship videos are also available at Christian book stores.

■ As a family, memorize a Bible passage each week for a quarter. You could introduce the idea by taking a few days and reading the chapter in *The Great Controversy* entitled "The Waldenses" for worship. Discuss what the chapter says about Waldensian youth memorizing all of Matthew and John plus the epistles (p. 80).

For another project as a family, memorize an entire Bible chapter and use worship time occasionally for a brief drill.

10. What about praying to the Holy Spirit?

I do not know of anything in Scripture against speaking to the Holy Spirit. Certainly He speaks often to us! I would think He would appreciate getting a vocal response. We pray to the Holy Spirit in hymns such as "Hover O'er Me, Holy Spirit" and "Sweet, Sweet Spirit."

11. How can I keep my mind from wandering when I pray?

Just this morning I talked to a busy mother of two who said, "I pray better if I write out my prayers."

Try it. It's a sure way to keep your mind from wandering! One possibility: write out a brief prayer using the acronym ACTS (adoration, confession, thanksgiving, supplication). Write a few sentences of adoration and of confession and of thanksgiving. Conclude with your requests. Then take that prayer and read it to God. Keep these prayers in some kind of notebook, and as God answers your requests, record the date and how He answered.

Before going to my present system, which I explained on pages 105-111 in the chapter "Finding Time to Pray," I used the ACTS pattern for about two years. But instead of writing out my prayers word-for-word, I outlined what I wanted to talk to God about on a three-by-five card, which I then used as I prayed. I generally kept the card in my shirt pocket and sometimes used it more than once during the day.

12. Is it important to kneel when you pray?

The Bible has many examples of people kneeling in prayer. Jesus, our Example, "kneeled down and prayed" (Luke 22:41). Of His disciples, it is recorded that they, too, "kneeled down, and prayed" (Acts 9:40; 20:36; 21:5).

Paul wrote, "I bow my knees unto the Father of our Lord Jesus Christ" (Ephesians 3:14). In confessing the sins of Israel, Ezra knelt (Ezra 9:5). Daniel "kneeled upon his knees three times a day, and prayed, and gave thanks before his God" (Daniel 6:10).

On other occasions, however, people didn't kneel. When Nehemiah prayed before he answered King Artaxerxes' question (Nehemiah 2:4), he obviously darted a prayer to heaven without even closing his eyes. Before calling forth Lazarus, Jesus stood before the tomb and "looked up" as He prayed (John 11:41).

My conclusion is that in both public and private worship, we should kneel whenever possible. But we can also cultivate the habit of talking to God as we come and go.

13. What about fasting? If I go without food, will God be more likely to answer my prayers?

No merit is earned by fasting. Yet in the Bible, fasting and prayer are sometimes mentioned together (Daniel 9:3; Mark 9:29, KJV). As outward evidence of their repentance, the people of Nineveh fasted in sackcloth and ashes (Jonah 3:5-10). David speaks of humbling himself by fasting (Psalm 35:13).

In His wilderness fast, Christ totally abstained from food. Another type of fasting consists of eating less or omitting desserts. On one occasion Daniel simply abstained for three weeks from what he called "pleasant bread" (Daniel 10:3, KJV).

Before God gave the Ten Commandments at Sinai, Moses asked husbands and wives to exercise self-denial by abstaining from sex during that time (Exodus 19:15). Paul suggested something similar when he wrote to the Corinthians, "Do not deprive each other except by mutual consent, so that you may devote yourselves to prayer" (1 Corinthians 7:5).

Also, for some, omitting the evening meal could provide extra time for study and prayer—as well as hleping to remove excess pounds.

Catherine Marshall suggests another kind of fast—one she drew from this verse: "So let us stop criticizing one another . . ." (Romans 14:13, Moffatt). She decided on a one-day fast in which she would not speak one word of criticism about anyone. Several times that day she had to suppress making pointed comments.

At a Bible study a few days later, Catherine shared her experience. The response, she says, was "startling." Many spoke of criticalness as one of the chief problems in their offices or in their marriages or with their teenage children.[1]

This could suggest other types of beneficial fasting: a "worry fast" (no worry for a week), or a "television fast" (a week with no TV). During the "television fast," you might add that amount of time to your allotment for Bible study and prayer.

Usable ideas

1. For a better understanding of the great controversy, read the chapter in *The Great Controversy* entitled "The Origin of Evil." As you read, put yourself in God's place. Ask yourself, "How would I have handled Lucifer's rebellion?

2. Try praying through several psalms one at a time. Read the psalm first, then talk to God about some of the content. If you love the out-of-doors, pray through one of the following nature psalms: 8, 19, 23, 65, 104.

3. Write out a sample prayer in which you use the ACTS pattern (adoration, confession, thanksgiving, supplication). Then find a quiet place and read it to God. Or, if you prefer, instead of writing your prayer, just talk to God about each of the four parts that ACTS represents.

For more information about using the ACTS pattern, I recommend Bill Hybel's *Too Busy Not to Pray*—a book being increasingly read around Andrews University. Just this week an Andrews student told me about a friend who said, "Reading that book really changed my life."

4. Take a one-week "television fast"—no television for a week. Use the TV time to read a Bible book.

Another possibility for using the time gained by the fast: Read parts of *The Great Controversy*. For an exciting chapter about the second coming of Christ, read "God's People Delivered."

There are powerful word pictures in almost every one of its forty-four paragraphs that would offer discussion possibilities within family worship times.

Notes

1. Catherine Marshall, "A Fast on Criticalness," from Leonard LeSourd's *Touching the Heart of God* (Grand Rapids, Mich.: Chosen Books, a division of Baker Book House, 1990), pp. 71, 72.

CHAPTER TWELVE

Intercessory Prayer— Anguish, Joy, or Both?

In *Yours for the Asking,* Edwin Gallagher writes:

> "When I was in my early teens I heard someone use the phrase *agonize in prayer.* I squirmed. *Agonize? In prayer?* It wasn't very appealing. The only agony in prayer that I knew was when the elder in our church kept us on our knees until I was sure that even the floorboards were aching (p. 48).[1]

Webster defines *intercession* as "prayer, petition, or entreaty in favor of another." Such intercession for others is a vital part of Christian living. In *The Ministry of Intercession,* Andrew Murray cautions against "praying constantly for ourselves." It's only through intercession for others, he adds, that we develop faith, love and perseverance (p. 31).

125

Benefits of praying for others include:

■ It ennobles the one who does the praying. In a book about the power of intercessory prayer—*Don't Just Stand There: Pray Something*—Ronald Dunn suggests, "We are never more like Christ than when we are praying for others" (p. 72).[2]

■ It enables God to work with greater power in the lives of those for whom we intercede.

Intercessory prayer, however, tends to be associated with a degree of agony. But can praying for others also be a joyous experience? Can it become something we do eagerly?

I'm discovering that it can. It should be prayed with deep concern, but through trust in Christ, it can also be enjoyable.

An important question

When you are praying for others, does the length of time you spend on your knees make a difference?

No one "earns credit" by the length of time he or she prays. As a monk, Martin Luther sometimes tried to pray all night. He then felt condemned when he would fall asleep.

It does, however, take adequate time to pray effectively. For one thing, as you pray for others, it is important that you also listen. I generally spend time with God's Word before praying. I prefer to hear from God before I say anything.

Often I also need to ask the "What?" kind of questions suggested earlier in this book on page 110. When praying for the conversion of an individual, I need to ask:

■ What sins in my life might be hindering this person's acceptance of Christ?

■ What's the next step in my relationship with this person? How can I have a more godly influence in his or her life?

Generally, the Holy Spirit, through the quiet voice of conviction, will suggest what you may need to do next.

Finding time for quiet thought and intercessory prayer is a challenge. It's got to be put into the schedule with a "whatever it takes" spirit. Otherwise, we will always be too busy.

Anguish and intensity

Here's another question some wonder about: Does successful intercessory praying depend on the anguish and intensity of the one praying?

We earn no credit by trying to make prayer an experience in agony. In some religious circles it appears that people try to work themselves up to a certain degree of emotion and intensity. In my opinion, that getting "worked up" resembles the prayers of the priests of Baal on Mount Carmel. In an attempt to get their god to answer, they shouted and even cut themselves "until their blood flowed" (1 Kings 18:28).

In contrast to this frenzy, Elijah's prayer must have taken less than a minute (see 1 Kings 18:36, 37). His prayer, though brief, was fervent. He prayed as if he knew God were listening.

In intercessory prayer, earnestness is vital. Listless prayers—or what one author calls "dribbled prayers"—are worthless. Consider this suggestion from *Christ's Object Lessons:*

> "We must not only pray in Christ's name, but by the inspiration of the Holy Spirit . . . When with earnestness and intensity we breathe a prayer in the name of Christ, there is in that very intensity a pledge from God that He is about to answer our prayer 'exceeding abundantly above all that we ask or think.' Eph. 3:20" (p. 147).

As for anguish, you cannot pray for someone you deeply love without feelings of deep concern. And the more unresponsive that child or spouse or friend appears to be, the deeper your concern will be. To expect anguish alone to make a difference, however, would be to depend on works.

Our great need is to pray with an implicit trust that blends faith and hope with the intensity.

"Powerful and effective"

"Pray for each other," James urges. "The prayer of a righteous man," he adds, "is powerful and effective" (James 5:16). As we noted earlier, we have no righteousness of our own with which to back up our requests. If you are like me, you sometimes have nagging doubts about even your worthiness to pray. The solution to that doubt is continual reliance upon the righteousness of Christ. It's in His righteousness that prayers are "powerful and effective."

"Elijah was a man just like us," James points out. "He prayed earnestly that it would not rain, and it did not rain on the land for three and a half years. Again he prayed, and the heaven gave rain, and the earth produced its crops" (James 5:17, 18).

James closes his remarks about prayer with this assurance:

> "My brothers, if one of you should wander
> from the truth and someone should bring him
> back, remember this: Whoever turns a sinner
> from the error of his way will save him from
> death and cover over a multitude of sins"
> (James 5:19, 20).

Prayer, then, can help turn a sinner from the error of his ways. It also helps sustain believers when difficulty and tragedy strike. At one point in his life, Job lost almost everything—his property, his children, his health. He longed for someone to pray for him and said, "I want someone to plead with God for me, as a man pleads for his friends" (Job 16:21).

Finding joy in intercessory prayer

How can we add both power and joy to the time we spend in intercessory prayer? Consider the following suggestions:

1. Do your intercessory praying at times when you are the most alert physically.

Fervency in prayer is largely dependent on physical vigor. As much as possible, schedule intercessory prayer for times when you are rested and refreshed.

2. For effectiveness, depend wholly on the merits of Christ rather than on the time spent or on the agony with which you pray.

Our most earnest prayers, apart from the righteousness of Christ, are worthless. As you pray, cling to Jesus, and depend totally upon His merits. This helps you pray in a confidence based on His goodness.

3. Be willing to make any changes needed in your own life that would enable God to better use you.

Sometimes the person doing the praying for a loved one is the biggest obstacle to that prayer being answered. Whatever the hurtful influences—unkind words, a critical attitude, no expression of appreciation, sloppy personal habits, et cetera—do whatever it takes to remove these hindrances in your own life.

We'll take a closer look at this in the chapter "Why Unanswered Prayer?"

4. Use promises of Scripture as you pray.

There are promises for your own needs, and promises that you can ask God to fulfill in the life of the person for whom you are praying. Why not underline these in your Bible? Then make it a habit as you pray to turn to one or more promises and talk to God about each. There's hope and optimism in the Bible promises.

5. After your regular prayer time, keep sending brief "whatever it takes" petitions to heaven during the day.

I am increasingly doing this with the Lord's Prayer. Sometimes I just make a quick mental survey of its petitions without praying the entire prayer. Then, if praying for Jim, I simply say, "Father, do whatever it takes to fulfill each of these petitions in Jim's experience today."

Jesus strongly emphasized that we are not heard because of "many words" (Matthew 6:7). But what does happen is this: when we "pray without ceasing," as Paul urges in 1 Thessalonians 5:17, we become more open to making needed changes in our own lives.

Praying "in the Spirit"

People sometimes ask, "What is praying 'in the Spirit'? Is it essential in intercessory prayer? And if so, how does one do it?" Paul speaks of the Holy Spirit as a major influence in effective prayer. "The Spirit helps us in our weakness," he writes. "We do not know what we ought to pray for, but the Spirit himself intercedes for us with groans that words cannot express" (Romans 8:26).

Caution about Pentecostalism makes some of us hesitant about what the Bible calls being "in the Spirit" (Romans 8:9). The worked-up emotion we associate with that kind of praying turns us off. We conclude that we don't want that during prayer or at any other time.

We need to remember this: An individual truly filled with the Holy Spirit will never be out of control. There will be none of what one author calls "fleshly displays of human emotion."

The Holy Spirit is a person. In his book *The Spirit and His Church*, Raymond Woolsey points out that in the New Testament the Holy Spirit has twenty-five different titles that indicate personality. He performs twenty different actions that only a personal being could carry out (p. 12).

The Holy Spirit is as real and as loving and as dependable as Christ Himself. If your eyes could be opened, you could see Him ready to walk through your front door to be with you in your home.

I have gone through John 14-16, where Christ spoke repeatedly about the Holy Spirit, and underlined each statement about Him. As I meditate upon these, I try to personalize each. In John 14:26, for example, Jesus speaks of the Holy Spirit as a Counselor. As I think about the Holy Spirit as a Counselor, or Comforter (KJV), I sense my need for His comfort and counsel.

As I understand it, praying in the Spirit is praying with an awareness of the Holy Spirit's presence. This depends on faith—not feeling—though at times you may sense the Holy Spirit as very close.

Often my greatest awareness of the Holy Spirit's presence comes when I am in the out-of-doors. When Philip found Nathanael and invited him to come see Jesus, the Saviour told him, "I saw you while you were still under the fig tree before Philip called you" (John 1:48). We too need outdoor locations where we can go to pray. In our Michigan back yard I find, not a fig tree, but Rose of Sharon trees, morning glories in bloom, or a plum tree that shades a portion of lawn on hot summer days.

"Filled with the Spirit"?

Paul speaks of being filled with the Spirit (Ephesians 5:18). What's that like?

Galatians 5:22, 23 mentions nine fruits of the Spirit—love, joy, peace, patience, kindness, goodness, faithfulness, gentleness, and self-control. I see being filled with the Spirit as the same as possessing the fruits of the Spirit. To be Spirit-filled is to be filled with love. And joy. And peace. And self-control. And with each of the other qualities listed.

Being Spirit-filled doesn't make a fool out of you. Rather, the Holy Spirit helps you act with compassion, in love, and with dignity.

For maximum enjoyment of conversation with God and Christ, we need to welcome the Holy Spirit into every aspect of our life.

Welcoming the Holy Spirit

Are you comfortable with thinking of the Holy Spirit as a person? Are you welcoming Him into your heart and home? Here are three suggestions:

1. Think of the Holy Spirit both as a person and as a very special Friend.

"I don't call you servants," Jesus said. "I call you friends" (see John 15:14, 15). The Holy Spirit likewise wants you for a very close friend.

2. Open your heart totally and completely to the Holy Spirit.

Ask your Friend to give you the mind of Christ (Philippians 2:5). Invite Him to help you love the things Christ loves and to hate the things He hates. Invite Him to possess you totally—to guide your thoughts, your words, and your acts.

3. Spend much time with God's Word.

Before opening God's Word, ask the Holy Spirit to enlighten your mind. His messages to you through the Word are as personal as if you heard an audible voice.

Usable ideas

1. Test the above suggestions about how to welcome more and still more of the Holy Spirit into your life. Do whatever it takes to cultivate a close friendship with the Holy Spirit.

2. For further insights about Jesus, the Father, and the Holy Spirit, study the ideas in John 14-16.

3. Read the commentary on John 14-16 that is found in the chapter in *The Desire of Ages* entitled "Let Not Your Heart Be Troubled." Have a pencil handy for underlining ideas you want to remember.

Notes

1. Edwin Gallagher, *Yours for the Asking* (Washington, D.C.: Review and Herald Publishing Association, 1978), p. 48.

2. Ronald Dunn, *Don't Just Stand There: Pray Something* (Nashville: Thomas Nelson Publishers, 1991), p. 72. Used by permission.

CHAPTER THIRTEEN

Making a Difference!

Intercessory prayer really does make a difference!

A young minister told the delegates at an academy Bible conference that during the first year of his ministry he saw only one person converted and baptized. And that one came from a Bible study started by the previous pastor. It finally dawned on him that he had been so busy that he wasn't doing much praying.

He decided to set aside ten minutes a day to intercede for others. The first morning he took off his watch, laid it on the bed, and began to pray. After praying for what seemed like ten minutes, he glanced at his watch. "I had prayed only three minutes," he told the delegates.

"I returned to my praying," he said. He emphasized that there is no merit in simply putting in time. Strength in prayer is better than length in prayer. But as he took time, He sensed the Holy Spirit at work in the lives of those for whom he was praying. Prayer was no longer a duty. It became a joyous privilege.

And at the end of his second year in the ministry he could look back on thirteen baptisms!

Jesus praying for people

The only record we have of Jesus praying for Himself was in Gethsemane. Ever and always, His praying seems to have been for people. Even in Gethsemane, before He prayed for Himself, He first prayed the prayer recorded in John 17.

He apparently looked down the ages and included us in that prayer. Referring to His disciples, He told God, "My prayer is not for them alone. I pray also for those who will believe in me through their message" (John 17:20).

That takes in us!

Matthew 14, compared with John 6, gives us an unforgettable picture of Jesus praying for people. The setting is this: In an attempt to get away for a little rest, Jesus and His disciples left Capernaum and crossed by boat to a secluded spot across the Sea of Galilee. A crowd was waiting as they docked their boat—a crowd that soon grew to 5,000 men plus women and children.

After a day of healing and teaching, Jesus used five small barley loaves and some fish to feed some 10,000 people. Then the crowd, with dreams of Christ setting up an earthly kingdom, tried to crown Him king. Jesus had not come for that purpose. He firmly dismissed the people, then sent His disciples back across the lake (John 6:14-21).

Prayer in the foothills

Matthew tells what happened next:

> "And when he had sent the multitudes away, he
> went up into a mountain apart to pray: and
> when the evening was come he was there alone"
> (Matthew 14:23, KJV).

As we watch, Jesus goes a few hundred feet up into the foothills. He kneels and begins to pray. Describing the kneeling form of Jesus, one author writes, "Deep emotion shakes that noble form as He keenly realizes the doom of the people he has come to save" (*The Spirit of Prophecy*, vol. 2, p. 266).

We soon realize that Jesus is sobbing as He prays. He prays for the disciples. He prays for the crowd that He had to so firmly dismiss. He prays for all the Hebrew people. He prays for the millions of lost people of the Roman Empire.

Instead of getting a hoped-for rest, Jesus had spent the day healing hundreds of people. He had spoken to a crowd of thousands. He dealt with an enthusiastic attempt to crown Him king. He had firmly sent away twelve angry disciples. Physically and emotionally, He must have been drained.

Yet He spent hours in intercessory prayer!

Motivation!

What motivated Jesus to pray so earnestly and with such deep feeling?

"I have loved you with an everlasting love," Jesus said through Jeremiah (Jeremiah 31:3). "Greater love has no one than this," He told the disciples, "than he lay down his life for His friends" (John 15:13).

So today intercessory prayer flows out from love. Because people matter to God, they matter to us. We don't see people as they are. We see them as they can become.

Christ had that kind of vision. He could glance ahead all the way into eternity. He saw the future of the people for whom He prayed—with millions upon millions of them in "the new earth" (Revelation 21:1). He saw them transformed in character and clothed with garments of praise and thanksgiving. He saw a world bathed in the light of heaven. He saw the years moving on in gladness. He heard the morning stars singing together and the sons and daughters of God shouting for joy.

This vision steadied His prayers. It can be the same for us. Zechariah gives us a preview of what intercessory prayer can help bring about:

> "The Lord their God will save his people in that day, as a Shepherd caring for his sheep. They shall shine in his land as glittering jewels in a crown. How wonderful and beautiful all shall be (Zechariah 9:16, 17, LB)!"

With a love for youth, Zechariah seems especially to notice the "young men and girls" who are there. He describes them as "radiant with health and happiness" (Zechariah 9:17, LB).

Prayer for our little ones

Through Christ, the potential for each newborn child is exactly what the preceding passage describes: a future "radiant with health and happiness."

At the birth of a little one, both parents start what should be continuous prayer for their family. Sondra Johnson asks, "Does any of us, when first beginning the adventure in motherhood, really realize that it will be a lifetime of prayer?"[1]

Along with private prayer for our children, devotional time with them is essential. Bible truth is like leaven (Matthew 13:33)—it's got to be within in order to work.

The minds of young children are so impressionable! If we expect to see our children grow up loving the Bible and loving God, we've got to plan time for devotion and prayer in our homes.

One blessing from family prayer time is the extra protection those prayers provide for us and our children. Satan complained to God about the hedge He put about Job and his possessions (Job 1:10). We can thank God for it! Every morning, before our children leave the house, let's put a hedge of faith and prayer about them.

Youth who pray

Through many years of Bible teaching in denominational schools, I have had opportunity to get acquainted with hundreds of students.

Many give evidence of having established good devotional habits. They pray earnestly and seek to win other youth to Christ.

In San Diego, an academy sophomore girl, for example, invited a sixth-grade boy in her neighborhood to attend church. He did. Then she helped arrange for him to attend San Pasqual Academy. While there, he decided to be baptized—all because of the concern and prayers of a neighbor girl who "adopted" him as a little brother.

As the preceding experience illustrates, youth often are best able to reach other youth. To each student reading this, let me suggest this: Begin a "Top Ten" prayer list on which you record the names of ten other youth you most want to be won to Christ. Build non-romantic friendships, and as appropriate share what you believe. As they show interest, invite them to services at your church.

Most important of all, begin to pray with a "whatever it takes" concern. See what God can do through your influence and prayers.

Youth who don't pray

Many youth in the church don't pray. Other interests seem to have crowded out the things that really count. There is no inclination to pray for and with each other.

Why?

To parents, I pose this question: Would our children do better spiritually if we established a more simple lifestyle? What's the real cost—the eternal cost—of extras like multiple television sets, boats, expensive vacations, the latest luxuries? Do we have such a passion for earning more money and buying more things that devotion gets crowded out?

If so, is it time for heart-searching and prayer? Are we modeling Christ's love and compassion and godly living? Are we helping youth gain a godly conscience of their own? Do they have strong convictions against drugs, alcohol, premarital sex, adultery, and similar temptations?

Unless we have a good system for monitoring television, would we be wise to exclude it from our homes? I know from experience that you can raise children without television. Our three—a daughter and two sons—had none while growing up, and now two of the three are raising their children the same way.

For homes that feel television is a must, I would ask this: What would happen if you limited television to no more than an hour a day and then gave equal time to family fellowship, study, and prayer?

Let's do whatever it takes to give our families every spiritual advantage! In our family, we have relied heavily on a promise in Isaiah 49. There, God asks, "Who can demand that a tyrant let his captives go?" He replies with this encouraging promise:

> "Even the captives of the most mighty and most terrible shall all be freed; for I will fight those who fight you, and I will save your children" (Isaiah 49:24, 25, LB).

Unconverted adult family members

Cain and Abel had similar parental guidance. One loved God; the other became a murderer. From Eden until now, parents have had to endure the anguish of seeing children turn their backs on God. As we noted earlier, here in North America alone, there are between a half million and a million young adults raised in the Seventh-day Adventist Church who have left it.

Let's not give up on them! The above promise from Isaiah 49 applies to them too! It's also a promise children can claim on behalf of non-Christian parents.

A number of authors, including Ellen White, refer to the prayers of Monnica, the mother of a rebellious son named Augustine. In a marriage arranged by her family, Monnica had been wed to an unbeliever. Augustine was the oldest of two sons.

During his youth and twenties, Augustine rejected Christianity. Historians picture him as a liar, a thief, and a womanizer. Like many young men today, he lived with a girlfriend. At nineteen he fathered a son.

In 1885 Ellen White wrote a three-page message to parents entitled "Parental Responsibility." It's mostly about helping children develop right habits and right ways of thinking. But in the closing paragraph, in the context of prayer, the author tells of Augustine's mother praying for her son's conversion. She had no evidence that the Spirit of God was doing anything, but she did not become discouraged:

> "She laid her finger upon the texts, presenting be-
> fore God His own words, and pleaded as only a
> mother can. Her deep humiliation, her earnest
> importunities, her unwavering faith, prevailed,
> and the Lord gave her the desire of her heart"
> (Ibid., pp. 322, 323).

The chapter closes with the suggestion that God still listens to His children's petitions.

> "If Christian parents seek Him earnestly, He will
> fill their mouths with arguments, and for His
> names sake will work mightily in their behalf in
> the conversion of their children" (Ibid., p. 323).

And for parents with an unbelieving spouse, here's further encouragement: long before the conversion of Augustine, Monnica's cantankerous husband was con-verted by his wife's prayers. He was baptized a few months before his death. Augustine was only seventeen when his father died. He was thirty-two when he was converted.[2]

Intercessory prayer for your pastor

"The greatest thing you can do for a pastor," someone has said, "is to pray for him."

At a large church of my acquaintance, the pastor gives duplicate messages three times each weekend. During each service a small group of intercessors meets to pray for their pastor.

Does this make a difference in the effectiveness of the worship service?

In 1872 Dwight Moody visited England for some rest. Someone prevailed upon him to speak to a church in London. It turned out to be a disaster. He got no response from his audience. They were cold. Dead.

A woman who had attended had an invalid sister at home. When she told her about it, the sister turned pale. "Mr. Moody from Chicago?" she asked. "If I had known he was going to preach this morning, I would have eaten no breakfast and spent the whole time he was preaching in prayer for him."

She then said, "Now, sister, go out of the room, lock the door, and send me no dinner; no matter who comes don't let them see me. I am going to spend the whole afternoon and evening in prayer!"

Moody had dreaded having to preach again that evening. E.M. Bounds, who shares this story, commented: "So while Mr. Moody stood in the pulpit that had been like an ice-chamber in the morning, the bedridden saint was holding him up before God, and in the evening God, who ever delights to answer prayer, poured out His Spirit in mighty power."

The church was packed, with a spiritual atmosphere pervading it. Said Moody, "The powers of an unseen world seemed to have fallen upon the audience." He decided to give an invitation for people to accept Christ as their personal Saviour. To Moody's amazement, 500 people stood. He repeated the invitation in an attempt to filter out any insincere respondents. But all 500 went forward to accept Jesus. A major revival followed.

Usable ideas

1. Space has not permitted discussion of any of the intercessory prayers of Paul, such as Ephesians 3:14-21 and Colossians 1:9-14. As you pray for friends or family members, consider sometimes including ideas from one or both prayers.

2. Consider developing a personal intercessory prayer list that you call "The Top Ten." On it, list the names of ten people you most want to see converted. In your morning prayers, ask God to do "whatever it takes" to bring them to Himself. As much as you can, keep them in mind during the day—and while you drive, walk, or work about the house or yard, send more "whatever it takes" prayers heavenward.

3. Pastor Bob Beltz, author of *Transforming Your Prayer Life,* tells about what he calls his "Miracle List." Requests in this list, he says, are "impossible apart from intervention by the living God." Above the list he has written Jeremiah 33:3 and Ephesians 3:20.

Why not develop a "miracle list" of your own? As you talk to God, you could include an appropriate promise with each request.

4. A suggestion to pastors: Whenever I have taught "The Ministry of Prayer" class at the Andrews University Seminary, our enrichment reading has been from the nine volumes of *Testimonies for the Church.* Hundreds of pages of this material deal either with ministry or with the devotional life. A considerable part of that is addressed directly to ministers.

You will find a lot of practical help for your own spiritual experience and for your ministry if you spend time with any of the messages listed by title at the end of this chapter. Lay members who read from these chapters will also find rich content with "high user value." I especially recommend

"Christ's Ambassadors" in volume 4 and "Looking to Jesus" in volume 5.

Volume 2:
"Appeal to Ministers" (334-346)
"Address to Ministers" (498-522)

Volume 4:
"Appeal to Ministers" (260-270)
"Address to Ministers" (313-320)
"Christ's Ambassadors" (393-407)
"The Servants of God" (523-537)

Volume 5:
"Looking unto Jesus" (199-202)
"Christian Growth" (263-272)
"Praise Ye the Lord" (315-319)

Volume 7:
"Family Worship" (42-44)
"Faith and Courage" (210-214)
"Take Time to Talk with God" (250-253)

Notes

1. Leonard E. LeSourd, *Touching the Heart of God* (Grand Rapids, Mich.: Chosen Books, a division of Baker Book House, 1990), p. 203. Used by permission.
2. Ibid., pp. 200-203.

CHAPTER FOURTEEN

Why Unanswered Prayers?

I magine yourself as a pollster who has been asked to do interviews about unanswered prayer. Examples that people share with you include:

- I'm praying for my son to become a Christian, but he's as rebellious as ever.

- I've been praying for my husband to stop drinking. He still comes home drunk every weekend.

- I asked God to heal my mother of cancer, but she died.

- I've been asking God to help me quit smoking, but it doesn't seem to do any good.

What unanswered prayers could you add to the preceding list?

Do you find that when you get answers to prayer, you tend to pray still more? But if you pray and pray and nothing happens, what then? Even if you don't doubt God's existence, you may be tempted to think that He isn't listening. "And if He isn't," you may conclude, "why pray?"

Why do many prayers go unanswered?

First, a few observations:

1. In our humanness, we can "ask amiss" (James 4:3, KJV)—selfishly, or with wrong motives.

The NIV for James 4:3 pinpoints one wrong motive:

> "When you ask, you do not receive, because you ask with wrong motives, that you may spend what you get on your pleasure" (James 4:3).

No sane parent gives a child every request. And in His mercy, God often denies that which would be hurtful to us.

2. It may be that we are not genuinely asking "in Christ's name."

In His teachings about prayer, Christ spoke of praying in His name more often than any other topic (see John 14:13; 14:14; 15:16; 16:23; 16:24). But what does that mean?

It's more than reciting "in Christ's name" at the end. The author of *The Desire of Ages* offers this insight:

> "To pray in Christ's name means much. It means that we are to accept His character, manifest His spirit, and work His works" (p. 668).

I like that! Praying in Christ's name includes the acceptance of His character—that is, His righteousness. Here's why I find much encouragement in that truth: In a passage about prayer in James 5:13-20, James assures us that "the prayer of a righteous man is powerful and effective" (James 5:17). I really do believe that. Yet a sense of my sinfulness has often kept me from claiming that promise. Then I remember: I can come to God clothed with the righteousness of Jesus Christ.

That's incredible! But it's true! When I trust the righteousness of Christ, for His sake I am counted righteous. His character stands in place of my character, and I am accepted before God just as if I had not sinned!

I'm so thankful for the grace and righteousness of Christ! Gratitude for Christ's righteousness makes me want to develop the spirit—attitude—of Christ. It encourages me to try to "work His works," that is, deeds of compassion and faith.

3. Sometimes our prayers are not answered because of wrongs in our lives that need to be corrected.

"If I had cherished sin in my heart," David wrote, "the Lord would not have listened" (Psalm 66:18). Let's look at some sins that can hinder what He wants to do for us:

The sin of self-sufficiency

"I will pour water on the thirsty land," God promises, "and streams on the dry ground" (Isaiah 44:3). Or, as Jesus put it, "Blessed are those who hunger and thirst for righteousness, for they will be filled" (Matthew 5:6).

Until we recognize our need, God is able to do very little. He has total power, but before He uses that power in my behalf, He strips away pride and self-sufficiency. To awaken that sense of need, He lets me struggle alone until I am ready to admit that I really do need His help.

The sin of self-will

"Sometimes I don't want God's will," a college girl declared. "I like the things that I'm doing!"

"You'll probably tell me," she said, "that sin never brings lasting pleasure. I know that. But some sins are fun while they last, and I don't want to quit."

When my personal preferences conflict with God's will, I find it helpful to remember that God's will is the ultimate in good living. Here's why: He always gives the best. The good things He wants us to experience include:

■ The forgiveness of sin.

■ Dependable guidance—the kind that helps us make decisions we'll never regret.

■ The power of the Holy Spirit to change us from the inside—developing love, joy, peace, patience, gentleness, goodness, humility, faith, self-control.

What more could I ask?

The sin of being half-hearted

"You will seek me and find me when you seek me with all your heart," God assures each of us (Jeremiah 29:13).

God asks for all my heart. Too often I hesitate to give Him everything. Yet that's so reasonable!

I still remember the evening in "the date room" of the girl's dorm at Union College when I asked a nineteen-year-old resident of that dorm to become my wife. I was nervous, and I don't remember my exact words. But I know what I didn't say. I did not say, "Sweetheart, I love you with almost all of my heart! I'm saving two percent for a girl I used to date."

The sin of robbing God

If it seems as if you aren't being heard when you pray, ask yourself, "Am I being honest with God?"

God once told His people, "Ever since the days of your forefathers you have turned away from my decrees and have not kept them." He then urged, "Return to me and I

A reason for unanswered prayer: When we neglect to bring God our tithes and offerings, He limits His blessings to us just in proportion as we limit our gifts to Him.

---

will return to you." Startled, His people asked, "How are we to return?"

God replied with a question: "Will a man rob God?" He then charged, "Yet you rob me."

"But how," they asked, "are we robbing you?"

"In tithes and offerings," God answered. "You are under a curse—the whole nation of you—because you are robbing me" (Malachi 3:7-9).

God then made this promise:

"Bring the whole tithe into the storehouse, that
there may be food in my house. Test me in this,
and see if I will not open the floodgates of
heaven and pour out so much blessing that you
will not have room enough for it" (Malachi 3:10).

Does the preceding passage suggest any changes? Consider this fact from Bible history: *When God's people returned
faithful tithes and generous offerings to Him, He fulfilled His standing
promise to pour out His blessings upon them. But when they neglected
to bring tithes and offerings, He limited His blessings to them just in
proportion as they limited their offerings to Him.*

That "just in proportion" deserves a second look!

The sin of an unforgiving spirit

The Lord's Prayer contains six petitions. Christ enlarged
on just this one: "Forgive us our debts as we also have
forgiven our debtors" (Matthew 6:12). He emphasized that
if we expect to be forgiven, we must forgive others
(Matthew 6:14, 15).

One time Peter came to Jesus and asked, "Lord, how
many times shall I forgive my brother when he sins against
me? Up to seven times?"

Jesus answered, "I tell you, not seven times, but seventy-
seven times" (Matthew 18:21, 22).

The idea of extending forgiveness seventy times in one
day overwhelmed the disciples. It led them to cry out,
"Lord, increase our faith! That's impossible without your
help!"

And it is until we go to the cross. If an unforgiving spirit
has been reducing what God can do for you, come with
me to the cross. Watch as Roman soldiers bring spikes and
nail each hand of Christ to the cross. Watch as His feet
are spiked to the rough timber.

See the cross lifted and dropped into the hole. Take a
long look at the gaping wounds. Watch as blood falls drop
by drop onto the rocks below. Listen as Jesus prays, "Father,
forgive them, for they know not what they do."

I find it a lot easier to be forgiving after I review a scene like that!

The sin of an uncontrolled appetite

What three-letter word appearing in Genesis 3 got Eve into trouble?

"The serpent beguiled me," Eve confessed, "and I did eat" (Genesis 3:13). The word *eat* or its derivatives is found thirteen times in the twenty-four verses of Genesis 3!

In the wilderness of temptation, Satan approached Christ with the same temptation: food (Matthew 4:2-4). And in his letter to the Philippians, Paul spoke of those whose god "is their stomach" (Philippians 3:19).

For many of us, could the pampering of appetite be one of the top reasons for unanswered prayer?

Our appetites were given to us by God. When under the control of good judgment, appetite is a blessing. God made foods—dozens and scores of varieties—for our enjoyment.

But many refined foods—candies, cakes, sugared cereals, soda pop, and so on—tend to weaken our resistance to disease. And a sure way to build up dangerous deposits of sludge (cholesterol) in one's arteries is to follow the American custom of getting thirty to forty percent of our calories from fat. If I eat this way, what right do I have to expect God to answer my prayers for good health or for anything else?

One author has suggested that if we gain the victory over wrong eating habits, we will find it easier to dismiss all other temptations. That victory depends upon the right use of a will strengthened by the grace of Christ.

Let's suppose, for example, that you find chocolates very tempting. You are at a social occasion. About mid-afternoon, someone starts around a box of chocolates. As it approaches you, you silently say, "I choose to give my will to Christ, and I choose to do it now."

Then as the person next to you hands you the box of chocolates, you prayerfully tell yourself, "I will believe, I do believe that God is my helper." With that, you hand the chocolates on to the next person.

In Christ, you will gain the victory every time! And what works for chocolates works with every other allurement.

The sin of broken relationships

In the business world, we tend to do whatever it takes to maintain good relationships. We'll be courteous even if the other person isn't. And we may have absolutely no affection for that individual!

How different at home! There, those we love the most often are treated the worst. That can hinder our prayers. Peter wrote to husbands: "Husbands . . . be considerate as you live with your wives, and treat them with respect as the weaker partner and as heirs with you of the gracious gift of life, so that nothing will hinder your prayers" (1 Peter 3:7).

In 1 Peter 3 the apostle also spoke to wives. He urged "a gentle and quiet spirit" (1 Peter 3:4).

Back in the 1870s, a certain pastor and his wife were not getting along well. This suggestion to both the husband and wife is now found in volume 4 of *Testimonies for the Church:*

> "By putting on the ornament of a meek and
> quiet spirit, ninety-nine out of a hundred of the
> troubles which so terribly embitter life might be
> saved" (p. 348).

Could that advice make a difference in how often you get answers to your prayers?

The sin of not hearing the cry of the poor

"If a man shuts his ears to the cry of the poor," Solomon wrote, "he too will cry out and not be answered" (Proverbs 21:13).

In Luke 12 Jesus told about a landowner blessed with good crops. As he harvested his abundance, he asked himself, "What shall I do with all this grain?"

"This is what I'll do," he said. "I will tear down my barns and build bigger ones, and there I will store all my grain and my goods. And I'll say to myself, 'You have plenty of good things laid up for many years. Take life easy; eat, drink and be merry'" (Luke 12:18, 19).

This farmer probably had a good reputation. He had worked hard. He had been honest. He may have started his day with a formal prayer. But God was not impressed. That night He went to this outstanding citizen and said, "You fool! This very night your life will be demanded of you. Then who will get what you have prepared for yourself?" (Luke 12:20).

This man could have cultivated a compassionate spirit. He could have shared his abundance with people in need. God probably would have given him even more abundance. As he reached out to help others, his prayers could have been answered again and again.

The sin of unbelief

David summarizes the history of the Old Testament Hebrew people in these few words: "They limited the Holy One of Israel" (Psalm 78:41, KJV).

How did they do this? "They did not believe God" (Psalm 78:22).

Unbelief is deadly. It tends to reason away even the most positive proof. It's contagious—just a few words of doubt, of unbelief, can contaminate. And often it seeks a following—it's the nature of unbelief to make itself felt and heard.

We will take a closer look at how to deal with unbelief in the next chapter.

Proverbs 4:18 suggests, "The path of the righteous is like the first gleam of dawn, shining ever brighter till the full light of day."

May that ever be our experience!

CHAPTER FIFTEEN

The Battle Between Faith and Unbelief

Jim stood on the edge of a cliff. In the early evening darkness, he tried to see down into what he took to be a deep canyon.

Suddenly, the earth beneath his feet crumbled. As he went over the edge, he grabbed hold of a small tree. Suspended in space, he yelled, "Is there anyone up there who can help me?"

The canyon was only a small ravine. A local resident calmly replied, "Just let go of the limb—you'll be OK."

Jim, unable to see that he would not drop far, clung desperately to the tree. Then he yelled, "Is there anyone else up there?"

It's a battle we all fight—the struggle between faith and unbelief. God commands—and we hesitate. A voice from above urges, "Have faith in God" (Mark 11:22). Unbelief responds, "Isn't there some other way?"

I recently went through all four gospels looking for two things:

■ Each mention or example of faith

■ Each mention or example of unbelief

I came to this conclusion: The battle between faith and unbelief is a major theme in all four gospels. It is especially noticeable in John. Throughout that gospel, Christ was constantly confronted by unbelief. In His ministry, He continually sought to establish faith.

The battle

Here's the first mention in John of unbelief: "He came to that which was his own, but his own did not receive him" (John 1:11).

And the first statement about faith: "Yet to all who received him, to those who believed in his name, he gave the right to become children of God" (John 1:12).

From that first mention in John 1, the record repeatedly brings either faith or unbelief into focus in chapter after chapter. In His talk to Nicodemus in John 3, Christ uses *believe* or *believed* seven times (vv. 12, 15, 16, 18).

In John 4, Christ met a woman at the well, who invited others to come see Him. He spent two days as their guest. When He left, they told the woman: "We no longer believe just because of what you said; now we have heard for ourselves and we know that this man really is the Savior of the world" (John 4:42).

We know! What a difference those words can make in the perplexities of life!

In John 6, after Christ's "bread of life" talk, seventy of His disciples "did not believe" (John 6:64). Of them, John wrote, "From that time many of his disciples turned back and no longer followed him" (John 6:66).

Two groups. In John 4, people who said, "We know that this man really is the Saviour." In John 6, a group that "did not believe."

And in every heart, two contenders. Unbelief calls out its troops, led by Satan, to cut us off from the Source of strength. Faith marshals its forces, led by the Author and

Finisher of our faith. Hour by hour the conflict rages—in what a 1901 article in *The Youth's Instructor* called "a hand-to-hand fight."[1]

Which will win in my life? Which in yours? That question each must decide for himself or herself.

Some facts about doubt and unbelief

Webster defines *doubt* as uncertainty of belief or opinion. Doubt tends to become unbelief—defined as incredulity or skepticism. That, in turn, often becomes disbelief—positive rejection.

The Pharisees saw the ministry of Christ as a threat to their position. Doubt quickly became unbelief, which soon hardened into outright rejection. From their experience, we can draw the following conclusions about disbelief:

1. Stifling one's conscience prepares the way for doubt and unbelief—and then disbelief—to take control.

John records that many of the rulers believed in Jesus but did not confess Him "for fear they would be put out of the synagogue" (John 12:42). As these men resisted the tugs of conscience, doubt became a skepticism that hardened into disbelief.

2. Disbelief reasons away even the most convincing evidence.

The resurrection of Lazarus should have convinced the Pharisees that Christ was no ordinary man. Yet in their blindness, they almost immediately got together to plan the death of Jesus (John 11:47-53).

3. Disbelief seeks a following.

The Pharisees repeatedly tried to turn people against Christ. They desperately wanted to keep people in their camp.

4. The real cause of doubt and disbelief, in most cases, is the love of sin.

Though outwardly religious, the Pharisees loved material gain. In their greed, they turned the temple into a cattle market (John 2:13-17). Love of money was behind their disbelief.

Some facts about faith

Faith can be defined as (1) trust, (2) complete confidence, (3) something that is believed with strong conviction.

Faith is more than belief, more than intellectual assent. "Even the demons believe—and shudder," James declared (James 2:19, RSV). He points out that faith must be accompanied by deeds of righteousness (James 2:20-26). Genuine faith yields to Christ and fixes the affections upon Him. It works by love and purifies the heart (Galatians 5:6).

Hebrews 11, the faith chapter, begins with this definition: "To have faith is to be sure of the things we hope for, to be certain of things we cannot see" (v. 1).

The following summary statement equates faith with trust, and directs attention to what faith does:

> "Faith is trusting God—believing that he loves us,
> and knows what is best for our good. Thus, in-
> stead of our own, it leads us to choose His way.
> In place of our ignorance, it accepts His wisdom;
> in place of our weakness, His strength; in place
> of our sinfulness, His righteousness. Our lives,
> ourselves, are already His; faith acknowledges
> His ownership and accepts its blessings" (*Educa-
> tion*, p. 253).

His wisdom in place of our ignorance! *His* strength in place of our weakness! *His* righteousness in place of our sinfulness! Acknowledgement of *His* ownership! Acceptance of *His* blessings!

What greater help could anyone ask? So much—so very much—can be ours through a simple trust in Jesus!

A primary cause for our failures

Glance back over the last ten years of your life. What have been your greatest victories? What have been your worst failures?

Don't linger long on your failures. But against that background, let's look in on two scenes from the life of David:

Scene one:

Day after day, Goliath has challenged the armies of Israel. Goliath "was over nine feet fall and wore bronze armor that weighed about 125 pounds and a bronze helmet. . . . His spear . . . head weighed about fifteen pounds" (1 Samuel 17:4-7, TEV).

A youth named David strides into camp. He listens to Goliath's boastful challenges to the Hebrew troops. He then goes to Saul and tells him, "Your majesty, no one should be afraid of this Philistine! I will go and fight him" (1 Samuel 17:32, TEV).

You know the story. With a sling and five stones, David kills Goliath. In the battle that ensued, Saul's troops drove out the invading Philistines. David's faith helped save the nation.

Scene two:

David is fleeing from the jealous Saul. He lives in constant fear of discovery. He temporarily loses his faith in God's care and tries to lie his way out of a tight spot.

David's lie in 1 Samuel 22 first led to the slaughter of eighty-five priests. The murderers then destroyed the city where the priests lived—putting to death the men, women, children, and infants who lived there (1 Samuel 22:18, 19).

Abiathar, a priest who escaped, found David and told him what had happened. Imagine David's anguish as he made this confession to Abiathar: "I am responsible for the death of your father's whole family" (1 Samuel 22:22).

When preparing the *Faith and Prayer* syllabus for my Workshop in Prayer class at Andrews University, I reread portions of Ellen White's *Patriarchs and Prophets*—a book with eleven chapters of commentary on the life of David. From the preceding story, the author draws a lesson that had much influence upon me as I prepared the syllabus: "Every failure on the part of the children of God is due to their lack of faith" (p. 657).

Do you see that as an accurate perception? Does it describe your situation too?

Words of encouragement

The context for the preceding quotation speaks of David's perplexity and distress as he fled from Saul. He nearly lost sight of his heavenly Father. Yet this experience helped him better realize his own weakness. It taught him an important lesson—the need to constantly depend upon God.

Are you, too, dealing with perplexities?

Be encouraged with this: The Holy Spirit still comes to us during times of sorrow and discouragement. He seeks to encourage the faint-hearted, strengthen the feeble, and impart courage to those who are going through difficulties. Even when we err, God deals gently with us. He patiently helps us get our feet back upon the solid ground of trust in Him and His Word.

Two "case studies"

The following case studies, while hypothetical, are similar to real life—perhaps to someone you know.

Case study one: Sue attended a Christian college. Her physical beauty attracted a number of non-Christians. One with considerable money won her affections. Dates with him became more important than Christ. Over the protests of parents and friends, she married him.

When children came, Sue began to respond to the gentle voice of the Holy Spirit. She started taking her little ones to church. She herself experienced a new conversion. Her husband resented the changes he began to see in her. This precipitated conflicts that eventually led to divorce.

Now a single parent, Sue is attempting to provide a secure home and a Christian education for her children. But the money never goes around. Tensions multiply— earning a living, visitation rights, children spending summer vacations with the father and his new wife, and on and on.

Case study two: Tom filled his teen years with parties, drugs, liquor, and taking out girls. One night while taking two girls to a football game, he had a head-on collision. He alone survived. The beer bottles found in the car helped send him to prison.

While there, he accepted Christ as his Savior. He attempts to share his faith with other prisoners. But he lives with remorse and regret.

If you know a Sue or a Tom, or someone similar to these two struggling people, perhaps you could encourage them with these two suggestions:

■ Don't let feelings of guilt steal away your peace. No matter how terrible your sins, probably none of them led to the death of eighty-five ministers and their families, the way David's did. If you have confessed your sin and done all you can to make things right, God is just as eager to forgive you as He was to forgive David. For your encouragement, read Psalm 51—the one David wrote as a confession after his adultery with Bathsheba and his murder of her husband. Seek the same repentance that David experienced.

The following promise is just for you:

> "Though your sins be like scarlet, they shall be
> as white as snow; though they are as red as crim-
> son, they shall be like wool" (Isaiah 1:18).

■ Like David, let your sin teach you the necessity of continual dependence upon God. Consider also what God may be saying for your future in the following parable.

A parable

Through the prophet Jeremiah, God used a loincloth, or as the TEV words it, a pair of men's shorts, to teach an important lesson. Jeremiah reports this incident:

"The Lord told me to go and buy myself some
linen shorts and to put them on; but he told me
not to put them in water. So I bought them and
put them on. Then the Lord spoke to me again
and said, 'Go to the Euphrates River and hide
the shorts in a hole in the rock.' So I went and
hid them near the Euphrates" (Jeremiah 13:1-3,
TEV).

Some time later, the Lord told Jeremiah to go back to
the Euphrates and get the shorts. He did, but found that
they had rotted.

God then told Jeremiah that the rotten shorts represented His people. In their stubborn rejection of Him and
in their worship of other gods, they had ruined themselves.
He then added:

"So then they will be like these shorts that are
no longer any good. Just as shorts fit tightly
around the waist, so I intended all the people of
Israel and Judah to hold tightly to me. I did this
so they would be my people and bring praise
and honor to my name; but they did not obey
me" (Jeremiah 13:10, 11, TEV).

Consider two truths this parable underscores:

1. God wants His people to cling to Him the way an
undergarment clings to the body.

2. If we don't cling to God, sin will erode our faith and
make us like a rotten pair of shorts.

Through Moses, God had repeatedly urged the Hebrew
people to "cleave" (KJV) or "hold fast" (NIV) to Him. Here's
one of four such pleas in the book of Deuteronomy: "Love
the Lord your God, to walk in all his ways, and to cleave
to him" (Deuteronomy 11:22, KJV). See also Deuteronomy
10:20; 13:4; 30:20.

Think how different the history of this planet would
have been if the Hebrew people had clung to God the way
an undergarment clings to the body!

Clinging to God

How does one cling to God? Here are two suggestions:

■ Embrace Jesus as your personal Savior at the beginning of each new day.

The word *embrace* means to clasp in the arms, readily and gladly. It means to hug, to cherish, to eagerly receive. Here's a prayer the author of *Steps to Christ* suggests for the start of a new day:

> "Take me, O Lord, as wholly Thine. I lay all my plans at Thy feet. Use me today in Thy service. Abide with me, and let all my work be wrought in Thee" (p. 70).

■ Develop a strong faith in God's Word and in its guidance and its promises.

In the next chapter we'll be focusing on the promises and the help found in them.

Usable ideas

May I make three suggestions?

1. Resolve to do "whatever it takes" to gain victory over doubt and unbelief in your life. If you have access to the little book *Steps to Christ*, you might want to read the chapter entitled "What to Do With Doubt." It has helped thousands to dismiss their doubts.

2. Go through John and mark each mention or example of belief in a distinctive color. Then, using a different color, do the same with each mention or example of doubt or unbelief.

You could then pray about your discoveries. Talk to God about each mention of believing; ask Him to make each a living reality in your life. Seek also for the kind of relationship with God that Jesus described in these words: "I always do what pleases Him" (John 8:29).

3. As you dress tomorrow morning, let the undergarment that you put on remind you to cling to God all day long. Strengthen that determination by kneeling at your bed and committing the day to Him. Determine that with His help, you will cling to Jesus through every difficulty or temptation.

Notes

1. Adapted from *Sons and Daughters of God,* p. 328.

CHAPTER SIXTEEN

Developing Unlimited Confidence in God

O n a scale of one to ten, with ten the highest, how would you rate the strength of your present faith in God?

Think for a moment about these words from our title: Unlimited confidence in God. Would you be willing to do whatever it takes to develop that kind of faith?

It will take strong motivation. Paul implies that perhaps we could gain that motivation from the "failures-of-faith" stories in the Old Testament. He writes:

"These things happened to them as examples and were written down as warnings for us, on whom the fulfillment of the ages has come" (1 Corinthians 10:11).

A "might have been"

For an example, let's turn time back nearly thirty-three

centuries. Two million people are about to cross over the Jordan into the Promised Land.

Moses, their leader, will soon die. Joshua has been appointed to take his place. Moses is giving the oration recorded in Deuteronomy 30.

He is telling that huge crowd what to expect in their new home. He begins with a summary of the blessings they can expect through faith and obedience to God's commands:

> "You will be blessed in the city and blessed in
> the country. The fruit of your womb will be
> blessed, and the crops of your land and the
> young of your livestock—the calves of your herds
> and the lambs of your flocks. Your basket and
> your kneading trough will be blessed. You will
> be blessed when you come in and blessed when
> you go out" (vv. 3-6).

Moses speaks of deliverance from all enemies and of God's blessing "on everything you put your hands to" (v. 8). He again mentions the condition: "If you keep the commands of the Lord your God and walk in his ways" (v. 9). He then returns to the "abundant prosperity" they can expect:

> "The Lord will open the heavens, the storehouse
> of his bounty, to send rain on your land in sea-
> son and to bless all the work of your hands. You
> will lend to many nations but will borrow from
> none. The Lord will make you the head, not the
> tail" (vv. 12, 13).

God planned that Israel should develop into the greatest nation on earth. He urged them to obey His "decrees and laws" in their new home. "This," He said, "will show your wisdom and understanding to the nations, who will hear about all these decrees and say, 'Surely this great nation is a wise and understanding people'" (Deuteronomy 4:6, 7).

Obedience to the health laws God had given, for

example, would have made them the healthiest people on earth. The Hebrews would have had none of the diseases that afflicted other nations (Exodus 15:26). They could have kept the vigor they experienced during their wilderness wandering. While they had been on their simple wilderness menu, "there was not one feeble person among their tribes" (Psalm 105:37).

What could have been

In the previous chapter, we noted that God used Jeremiah and a pair of his shorts to show our need to cling to God in humble faith. Let's imagine that the Hebrew people had done so. Then picture yourself as a merchant in a country that was a neighbor of Israel. After the Hebrews are established in Canaan, you make a business trip that takes you through that land.

You discover prosperity everywhere. Everyone you meet reflects cheerfulness and contentment. You've never seen so many handsome, strong men or so many beautiful women!

You start asking questions. You learn that these people never get sick! You can't find a cripple or anyone sick in the whole nation!

And families are obviously happy! Husbands and wives get along. Children respect their parents! Lying, cheating, and stealing are almost nonexistent.

Would you go back home, contact some government officials, and urge that they send a delegation to Israel to find out the secrets of the country's prosperity? Would you also suggest that a team of physicians go there to find out how people stay so healthy?

The prestige that the Hebrew people would have gained in the eyes of other nations would have given them a far-reaching influence. The author of *The Desire of Ages* suggests that Jerusalem could have become "the mighty metropolis of the earth. From her walls the dove of peace would have gone forth to all nations. She would have been the world's diadem of glory" (p. 577).

That never happened.

Why? What kept the Hebrew people from the promised prosperity? What cheated them out of their potential greatness?

The 78th Psalm was written some 300 years after Moses. It tells the history of the Hebrew people up to that time—a history of disobedience and rebellion. In one sentence, David pinpoints the reason for their failures: "They did not believe in God or trust in his deliverance" (Psalm 78:22).

By their unbelief, "they limited the Holy One of Israel" (Psalm 78:41, KJV). They cheated themselves!

Are you and I doing something similar? What added blessings might we gain if we would develop "unlimited confidence in God"?

For a start toward developing that kind of faith, let's note a few incidents from the life of Christ.

Christ's focus on faith

"Have faith in God," Jesus urged (Mark 11:22). Again and again in His ministry, Christ either appealed for faith or commended faith. Note these examples:

■ Mark 4 tells about Jesus and the disciples getting caught in a storm on Galilee.

> "Waves broke over the boat so that it was nearly swamped. Jesus was in the stern, sleeping on a cushion. The disciples woke him and said to him, 'Teacher, Don't you care if we drown?' He got up, rebuked the wind and said to the waves, 'Quiet! Be still!' Then the wind died down and it was completely calm." (vv. 37-39).

> "Jesus then said to the disciples, 'Why are you so afraid? Do you still have no faith?'" (v. 40).

■ In Mark 5 a synagogue ruler asked Jesus to come heal his dying daughter. As they were going to the ruler's house, some messengers rushed up and told him, "Your daughter is dead." Jesus told the ruler, "Don't be afraid. Just believe" (Mark 5:36).

Just believe. A few minutes later, Jesus took the twelve-year-old girl by the hand and told her, "Little girl, I say to you, get up!" And she did (Mark 5:41, 42).

■ In Matthew 17 the disciples failed to heal a demon-possessed boy. In their frustration, they asked Jesus, "Why couldn't we drive it out?" Jesus replied, "Because you have so little faith" (Matthew 17:19, 20).

Christ went on to suggest:

> "If you have faith as small as a mustard seed,
> you can say to this mountain, 'Move from here
> to there' and it will move. Nothing shall be im-
> possible to you" (Matthew 17:20).

■ In Mark 5 a woman who had been subject to bleeding for twelve years had exhausted her funds on doctors who hadn't been able to help her. One day, as a crowd surrounded Jesus, she got close enough to touch His cloak and was immediately healed. Jesus asked, "Who touched me?" Trembling with fear, she fell at His feet and told Him everything. "Daughter, your faith has healed you," He gently told her. "Go in peace and be free from your suffering" (Mark 5:34).

"Educate yourself to have unlimited confidence in God," the author of *In Heavenly Places* suggests (p. 71).

Confidence is defined as bold certainty; consciousness of feeling sure; being certain.

Unlimited means no limits; boundless; infinite.

Can one develop a boundless faith? Can you develop a faith that is almost infinite? And if so, how? What does it take to develop "unlimited confidence in God"?

A curriculum for building faith

Did you notice the word *educate*? Educate yourself to have unlimited confidence in God.

Paul puts it like this: "Faith comes from hearing the message, and the message is heard through the word of Christ" (Romans 10:17). The key element for an educated faith is "the word of Christ."

Perhaps Christian college curriculums should include a major entitled "Developing Unlimited Confidence in God." If you were planning courses for such a curriculum, what classes would you consider needful?

Probably none of us will ever be called to develop such a curriculum. But in your own experience, would you like to develop a home-study plan for developing "unlimited confidence in God"?

I'd like to suggest four "courses" that I would include for a college curriculum. We'll look at the first three in this chapter. Then in the following chapter, I will suggest one more. Perhaps you can use at least some of these suggestions to help you develop a "home study" plan for your own use.

1. Get to really know Jesus.

Faith is Person-centered. In this course I would want my students to really get to know Jesus. We would seek a clear picture of what He is like. Questions I would want students to consider would include:

1. Is Jesus the kind of person you can trust? Is He dependable?

2. What qualities do you find in Jesus that you really admire? Is He someone you can safely love?

3. Can you safely give Him your heart, your will, your self?

Our textbook for this course would be the Gospels—especially John. For enrichment reading, I would suggest the book *The Desire of Ages.*

As a study technique, I would recommend the following:

> "It would be well for us to spend a thoughtful hour each day in contemplation of the life of Christ. We should take it point by point, and let the imagination grasp each scene, especially the

closing ones. As we thus dwell upon His great sacrifice for us, our confidence in Him will be more constant, our love will be quickened, and we shall be more deeply imbued with his Spirit" (p. 83).

Note especially this: "Let the imagination grasp each scene."

For doing this, I like to read a verse or passage from the Gospels that describes a single scene. If *The Desire of Ages* has any description applicable to that scene, I read it also. I then use the information gained to ask three questions: (1) What is there to see? (2) What is there to hear? (3) What is there to feel?

Notice the first of the three benefits mentioned above: "Our confidence in Him will be more constant."

2. Test God's promises

Paul suggests in Romans 12:3 that God gives every person a "measure of faith." Faith grows as it is exercised in appropriating the Word of God. In order to strengthen faith, we must often bring it into contact with the Word.

Peter writes of the abundant help available to us through God's Word:

> "His divine power has given us everything we
> need for life and godliness through our knowl-
> edge of him who called us by his own glory and
> goodness. Through these he has given us his very
> great and precious promises, so that through
> them you may participate in the divine nature
> and escape the corruption in the world caused
> by evil desires" (2 Peter 1:3, 4).

In my Workshop in Prayer class we systematically underline eighty of the better-known Old Testament promises and eighty from the New Testament. We also underline fifty of what I call command-promises.

I see all Bible commands, including the Ten Commandments, as command-promises. My logic is this: Whatever God asks us to do, He will help us do. In the commandment, "You shall have no other gods before me" (Exodus 20:3), I see God promising, "I will help you to put Me first."

In an attempt to help students readily find and use these statements, we underline and discuss them book by book. The largest number of Old Testament promises that we use come from Genesis, Exodus, Deuteronomy, Psalms, Proverbs, and Isaiah. In the New Testament, most come from Matthew, John, the letters of Paul, 1 John, and Revelation.

Like Webster, I define a promise as "a declaration that one will do or refrain from doing something specified."

Here's a Bible example of the former: "I will help you to speak, and will teach you what to say" (Exodus 4:12).

And this would be an example of a promise not to do something:

> "If you listen carefully to the voice of the Lord
> your God and do what is right in his eyes, if you
> pay attention to his commands and keep all his
> decrees, I will not bring on you any of the dis-
> eases I brought on the Egyptians, for I am the
> Lord, who heals you" (Exodus 15:26).

Here are samples of command-promises from the writings of Paul:

- "Be filled with the Spirit" (Ephesians 5:18).

- "Do everything without complaining or arguing" (Philippians 2:14).

- "Rejoice in the Lord always" (Philippians 4:4).

In these commands I see God as promising, "I will help you become Spirit-filled," "I will help you to not complain," "I will help you to always rejoice."

In a college class, I would want students to do the following with the promises and command-promises that they studied:

a) Learn to find them quickly in an underlined Bible.

b) Study each one carefully and note within the promise or its context any conditions that need to be fulfilled in order for God to do as He promises.

c) Systematically test individual promises. Ask God's help in fulfilling any conditions, and then ask Him to fulfill what He has promised.

3. Talk faith

One could include a number of "how-to" suggestions in a course about how to always speak with faith and hope. Here's one such suggestion: *When you encounter a mountain of difficulty, don't focus on the mountain; look, instead, to the Mountain Mover. Talk about God's power, not about the size of the mountain. Talk courage, talk faith, talk hope.*

Bible passages in which Jesus talks about mountain-moving faith include Matthew 17:20, Matthew 21:21, 22, and Mark 11:23.

In a faith-building course, I would have students spend some time in the book of Hebrews. I would want them to see Christ as our High Priest. Within that context, Paul writes more about faith than in any other epistle. He even suggests that we can be bold as we approach God with our requests (Hebrews 4:16, KJV). Here's that encouragement as worded in the NIV:

> "Therefore, since we have a great high priest who has gone through the heavens, Jesus the Son of God, let us hold firmly to the faith we profess. For we do not have a high priest who is unable to sympathize with our weaknesses, but we have one who has been tempted in every way, just as we are—yet without sin. Let us therefore approach the throne of grace with confidence, so that we may receive mercy and find grace to help us in our time of need" (Hebrews 4:14-16).

Often the worst of all "mountains" is the accusing of our

own conscience. While developing a Workshop in Prayer syllabus, I came across a comment on 1 John 2:1 which presents Christ as our Advocate. It points us, not to our guilt, but to Christ as our Defending Lawyer:

> "Satan stands at our right hand to accuse us, and our Advocate stands at God's right to plead for us. He has never lost a case that has been committed to Him. We may safely trust our Advocate; for he pleads His merits in our behalf"
> (Ellen White comments, *SDA Bible Commentary*, vol. 7, p. 948).

He has never lost a case that has been committed to Him! I tell my students, "That's the kind of lawyer to get when you know you are guilty." And it's an excellent basis for unfailing confidence in God!

A twice-a-day reminder

In my devotional study last summer I spent several weeks with just four Bible chapters: Jeremiah 30 through 33. My several "something new" discoveries—new to me at least—included:

■ These four chapters are in the context of a terrible apostasy by Israel—yet they are filled with some of the most faith-building promises in the Bible. The first part of Chapter 30 speaks of "the time of Jacob's trouble" (v. 7). But that is followed by gracious promises about God's ability to transform and save.

■ The second thing I discovered was a twice-daily reminder that God and His promises are totally dependable. God points to the certainty of the daily return of day and night as evidence of His dependability—and He does it not once, but three times (Jeremiah 31:35, 36; 33:19-21; 33:25, 26).

To make Himself unmistakably clear, God challenges readers to break the decrees that rule the day and night. If you can break them—"so that day and night no longer come at their appointed time" (Jeremiah 33:20)—then His promises to David can be broken.

In Jeremiah 33, God promises that David's throne and Jerusalem will be preserved for all eternity. He then explains how that will be:

> "I will make a righteous Branch sprout from David's line; he will do what is just and right in the land. In those days Judah will be saved and Jerusalem will live in safety. This is the name by which it will be called, The Lord Our Righteousness" (Jeremiah 33:15, 16).

Christ is that Branch. Christ is "The Lord Our Righteousness." And every promise He has given is as certain as the daily return of morning and evening!

Do you want a basis for "unlimited confidence in God"? Let each dawn and dusk be reminders that our God is totally trustworthy.

A "home study" curriculum

Many readers of this book will not be college students. And even those who are won't find a college that offers a major entitled "Developing Unlimited Confidence in God."

Let me therefore suggest a home study plan:

1. Really get to know Jesus. Study a gospel of your choice. If you have access to the biography of Christ called *The Desire of Ages,* also spend a few minutes with it each day.

As you read your Bible, linger on each scene and ask, What is there to see? What is there to hear? What is there to feel? Use your imagination to fill in details. As you do, the scene will become more real to you.

2. Regularly test God's promises. The Appendix has references to forty of the better-known Old Testament promises and forty New Testament promises. It also has references to twenty command-promises. Most promises are chosen from these books: Genesis, Psalms, Proverbs and Isaiah in the Old Testament; Matthew, John, Paul's epistles, and 1 John in the New Testament. Most commands are from the writings of Paul. Using a distinctive color, underline each of these eighty statements.

Then, a book at a time, meditate upon them. Ponder them over and over and talk to God about them. One by one, ask Him to fulfill each for you.

3. Develop the habit of talking faith. When you face a mountain-like problem, keep your eyes on the Mountain Mover. Don't dwell any more than necessary on the problem.

4. Let each dawn and dusk become reminders of God's dependability. Join me in making it a habit to pause for a moment to look at the eastern sky in the morning. Pause again, when possible, to watch the sunset or the coming of dusk. In both, hear God saying, "Trust Me. I am as dependable as the coming of morning and evening."

CHAPTER SEVENTEEN

Putting Praise Into Daily Living

I have just returned from attending a funeral for a high-school student killed in a car accident. At the service, the priest mentioned that the family had buried this young man's great-grandmother two days earlier. "It's hard to understand," he said, "why a young man of fifteen would also die."

He then directed attention to John 11 and to Christ's words to Martha as she grieved the loss of her brother. "I am the resurrection and the life," Jesus had told Martha. "He who believes in me will live, even though he dies" (John 11:25).

As I drove home, I recalled a statement of Jesus that began, "If I had not come . . ." (John 15:22). I asked myself, "What would life be like if Jesus hadn't come?"

At the time of Christ's birth, faith had grown dim even among the Hebrews. Hope had almost vanished. Death was an awful mystery. Most of the secular philosophers of that day apparently believed that "life is like a flake of snow, fallen on the river, for a moment white, then gone forever."

Then Jesus came! "The Word became flesh and made his dwelling among us," John wrote. "We have seen his glory, the glory of the One and Only, who came from the Father, full of grace and truth" (John 1:14).

And because of that we have reason for faith and hope—and gratitude—at a funeral!

The wonder of Christ's incarnation

"The Word became flesh." Jesus Christ, the Co-Creator of hundreds of billions of galaxies, became flesh! That fact alone gives reason for deep gratitude and unceasing wonder!

Paul calls it a "mystery"—God "manifested in the flesh" (1 Timothy 3:16). Believers speak of it as "the most marvelous thing that ever took place in earth or heaven—the incarnation of the Son of God."

One writer suggests that in contemplating that wonder, "we stand baffled before an unfathomable mystery, that the human mind cannot comprehend. The more we reflect upon it, the more amazing does it appear."

In our imagination, let's go back and watch it happen.

Time: late 5 B.C. or early 4 B.C.

Place: possibly a garden.

Occasion: the three Executives who run the universe are spending the last minutes they will have together for several decades.

What they are about to do has not been an easy decision for any of them. As they stand there, with the incarnation only minutes away, they silently review the events that have led to this moment—the rebellion of Lucifer, the creation of the earth, the sin of Adam and Eve, the first lamb sacrificed in Eden, the ministries of the prophets, the failures of the Hebrew people, the rise and fall of empires, the emptiness and sorrow in human hearts.

The silence deepens. For Jesus, there is loneliness and pain ahead—and much risk. Lucifer will try to destroy Him almost as soon as He is born. Failing that, he will continually attempt to get Jesus to sin.

For the Father also, the next thirty-three years hold

loneliness and pain and risk. If Jesus fails in His mission, if He sins, He will eventually become associated with Lucifer. And then what? Will both eventually have to be destroyed? Would the universe itself survive?

And the Holy Spirit? He doesn't fear the attempts Herod will make to destroy the infant Jesus. A single angel can take care of that. But what if Jesus falls into even one sin? What then?

Do they really want to go through with it? Are they risking too much?

The final moments

They have discussed this before. Though silent, each reaffirms the decision made earlier. The human race is worth the risk! If only one person is saved from eternal death, it will be worth all the risk, pain, and suffering.

The Father steps over to Christ. His eyes fill with tears as He embraces Him. "Goodbye, Son."

The Holy Spirit clasps the hand of Christ. "I'll be with you every step of the way," He says quietly.

What happened next cannot be described. Scripture only tells that it happened. "The Word became flesh." Perhaps a cloud enveloped the Son. Perhaps there was a flash of light. Within that cloud or flash of light the co-Creator of the galaxies was compressed into a single cell. By the Spirit, that cell was then implanted into Mary's womb.

Eventually, Mary had to share the story of her pregnancy with Joseph. We can understand why he doubted Mary's story. He knew where babies came from. Even the *National Enquirer*, had there been one in Jerusalem, wouldn't have accepted a story like Mary's.

But then an angel appeared to Joseph in a dream. "Joseph, son of David," he said, "do not be afraid to take Mary home as your wife, because what is conceived in her is from the Holy Spirit. She will give birth to a son, and you are to give him the name Jesus, because he will save his people from their sins" (Matthew 1:20, 21).

Salvation from sin! What greater blessing could heaven give? What greater reason for fervent praise?

Life purchased with blood

"In him was life," John said of Jesus, "and that life was the light of men" (John 1:4).

Peter spoke of the cost of that life.

> "You know that it was not with perishable things such as silver and gold that you were redeemed from the empty way of life handed down to you from your forefathers, but with the precious blood of Christ" (1 Peter 1:18, 19).

And as Del Delker sometimes sings, "Each drop of blood bought me a million years." That's an eternal reason for gratitude and praise!

One time Dwight Moody commented: "It is life that men want and value most. If a millionaire on a sinking vessel could buy another six months of life, he would give

---

Let 80 years be represented by the 16 waking hours of a day, and the time clock of life looks like this:

At age 10, it was 8:00 a.m. for you.
At age 20, it's 10:00 a.m.
At age 30, it's time for lunch.
At age 40, it's 2:00 p.m.
At age 50, it's 4:00 p.m.
At age 60, it's time for supper.
At age 70, it's 8:00 p.m.
At age 80, it's time for lights out.

---

his millions in an instant." Yet how few show the same concern for eternal life!

In Psalm 90 David wrote: "Seventy years is all we

have—eighty years, if we are strong; . . . life soon is over, and we are gone" (v. 10, TEV). He then suggests this prayer: "Teach us how short our life is, so that we may become wise" (v. 12, TEV).

When I was teaching at Glendale Adventist Academy, one year in a speech contest a senior class president developed this thesis: "Man was made for eternity." That is so true! "At one time or another," Edwin Teale wrote, "there comes to most of us a realization of how much will remain undone when the world ends for us."

"Even if we circle the globe," he went on, "how many sights and sounds and smells we still shall miss! Even if we become acquainted with millions, how many possible friends we never shall know!"[1]

We were made for eternity! We were designed to ever increase in knowledge and wisdom! We were intended to ever explore new fields of thought and to forever discover new wonders. We were made to ever increase in the capacity to know and to love and to enjoy. And even as the joys increase, we will know that ahead lies still more love and joy.

The thought that Jesus died on a cross to obtain these infinite privileges for us seems almost unbelievable—and especially when we recall His pre-incarnation position and dignity!

Ella M. Robinson, a granddaughter of Ellen White, shared this illustration from her grandmother:

> "Once I heard her say that if it were possible to
> think of a person in such sad circumstances that
> he had no earthly thing to be thankful for, still
> he had the hope of salvation; that was enough to
> keep him singing from morning till night"[2]

More and still more!

After presenting the wonder of the incarnation in John 1:14, the writer also added, "Out of the fullness of his grace he has blessed us all, giving us one blessing after another"

(John 1:16, TEV). God has a reserve of so many blessings that it will take "the coming ages" for Him to "show the incomparable riches of his grace"—grace which He has expressed through "his kindness to us in Christ Jesus" (Ephesians 2:7).

As we consider these blessings, we could fill every day with gratitude and praise. I want to learn to do this even when things go wrong. Consider something I recently discovered:

Jeremiah ministered during one of the gloomiest periods in the history of God's people. During that last forty years of Judah's existence as a nation, the sins of the leaders and people were taking the nation toward disaster and ruin. For the faithful few, the future was dark indeed.

I was amazed, therefore, when I learned from Jeremiah 33:11 that during that dark period, the people were urged to "bring the sacrifice of praise into the house of the Lord." Paul used similar wording when he said, "Through Jesus, therefore, let us continually offer to God a sacrifice of praise" (Hebrews 13:15).

Continual praise!

Think again about a college major (or home-study course) entitled "Developing Unlimited Confidence in God." If I were designing the curriculum, I would want to include a course about learning to praise God even in the midst of difficulties and loss.

The benefits of expressing gratitude include:

1. It tends to increase your faith.
2. It gives you more power in prayer.
3. It steadily increases your love for God.
4. God gives you still more for which to praise Him.

From darkness to light

Here's one objective I would suggest for a class learning to praise God: Seek a growing appreciation for the light and beauty brought to us by Jesus.

At the birth of John the Baptist, his father Zechariah compared the coming of the soon-to-arrive Messiah to the sunrise. "Our God is merciful and tender," he said. "He will cause the bright dawn of salvation to rise on us and to shine from heaven on all those who live in the dark shadow of death, to guide our steps into the path of peace" (Luke 1:76-79).

Physical light brings so many blessings! The light shining from the face of Jesus is even more beautiful.

Physical light, for example, is essential for beauty! We see its results in the greens of meadow and forest, in the color of tulips and roses, in the gold of a grain field, in the blush of the ripening peach, in the red of the apple, and, yes, in the color in your cheeks.

So in the Christian life. Light produces beauty of character—and a beauty seen in the face as well. Fellowship with Christ does something to your face that goes deeper than physical beauty. "Look to him," David invites, "and be radiant" (Psalm 34:5, RSV).

The light of the sun is also synonymous with joy. After a week of clouds in winter, have you noticed what happens to your spirits when the sun breaks through?

Something similar happens when the Sun of Righteousness breaks through. There is healing in the light of His presence. Malachi compares it to the exuberance of calves that have just been released from their dark stalls to go out into the springtime sun (Malachi 4:2).

Physical light is essential for fruitfulness. It adds to a sense of security. It is essential for life. And there are parallels in the spiritual world—the fruits of the Spirit, security in Christ, and life itself. All come through knowing and loving Christ. "For with you," David writes, "is the fountain of life" (Psalm 36:9).

Recording answers to prayer

A class in which students learned to praise God would do well to develop some system for recording prayer requests—and answers to those requests.

During Samuel's leadership, the Hebrew people had met at Mizpah to seek the Lord in repentance and prayer. The

Philistines learned about this meeting and organized an attack. In their fright, the people asked Samuel to pray for them (1 Samuel 7:8).

As Samuel prayed and offered a lamb, "the Lord answered him" (v. 9). While the first enemy troops were drawing near "to engage Israel in battle," the Lord "thundered with loud thunder against the Philistines and threw them into such a panic that they were routed before the Israelites" (1 Samuel 7:10). The Israelites destroyed many of the invaders as they chased them back to their own country.

Samuel then set up a stone and named it Ebenezer, saying, "Thus far has the Lord helped us" (1 Samuel 7:12). Drawing a lesson from this, Ellen White speaks of humble believers who seek to win others, and says:

> "Let such ones keep a diary and when the Lord gives them an interesting experience, let them write it down as Samuel did when the armies of Israel won a victory over the Philistines" (*SDA Bible Commentary*, vol. 2, p. 1012).

"Every tear that the Lord has helped you wipe away from sorrowful eyes," she further suggests, "every fear that has been expelled, every mercy shown,—trace a record of it in your diary" (Ibid.).

This suggestion is directed to laymen who are attempting to help their neighbors. It's a good suggestion for pastors, too. It can help restore courage when one encounters resistance to the Gospel. Let what God has already done awaken gratitude and praise as you plead for Him to again work with life-changing power.

It is for our own benefit to keep some kind of record of God's gifts and of His answers to our prayers. When a need or problem arises, we can glance back through our journal and review what God has done. As we recall these blessings and give thanks for them, faith will be strengthened to claim and receive more and still more.

Blessings numerous as raindrops

The book *Messages to Young People* contains this illustration from the world of nature for young people to consider. It mentions the mercies that surround us every moment and then suggests:

> "Let the precious blessings of God awaken gratitude in you. You cannot number the blessings of God, the constant loving-kindness expressed to you, for they are as numerous as the refreshing drops of rain" (p. 409).

The precious blessings of God! As numerous as the refreshing drops of rain!

I think of this almost every time we get a Michigan thunderstorm! Our home is built upon a 100 by 150 foot lot (a third of an acre). Sometimes I try to imagine how many raindrops fall upon our property every second! God's blessing are that superabundant!

Ideas to test

1. John 1 contains nine different titles and names for Jesus. Take a little devotional time to underline these and then ask, "What additional reasons for praising Jesus do I find in these titles and names?"

2. If you haven't already done so, begin a simple system of journaling that includes recording your prayer requests. Record also the answers as they come.

3. The next time you experience a summer rainstorm, think of the *Messages to Young People* illustration given above.

4. Evaluate this suggestion:

> "If the loving-kindness of God called forth more thanksgiving and praise, we would have far more power in prayer. We would abound more and more in the love of God and have more bestowed to praise Him for" (*Testimonies for the Church*, vol. 5, p. 317).

Over a thirty-day period, test the assurance that if we praised God more, we would love Him more and also "have more bestowed to praise Him for."

5. As you start a prayer, sometimes read aloud to God an expression of adoration and praise from a psalm. (Just in the last fifty psalms, you will find expressions of adoration in these: 103-108, 111-113, 117, 118, 134-136, and 144-150).

Notes

1. Quoted by Mary Covey O'Neil, "Life Is Too Short," *Signs of the Times,* Feb. 15, 1965, p. 7.

2. *The Youth's Instructor,* Mar. 23, 1948, p. 10.

CHAPTER EIGHTEEN

Mighty Petitioners With Mighty Arguments

Capernaum had never seen anything like it! Immediately after sundown, every sick person, every cripple, every blind person in the city had shown up at Peter's front door! Some came leaning upon staffs, some supported by friends, some carried on couches.

Hour after hour they came—and Jesus healed every one. The night air was filled with shouts of triumph and of deliverance.

The excitement had started at the synagogue that Sabbath morning. A madman, shouting at the top of his voice, had rushed in as Jesus was speaking. "What do you want with us, Jesus of Nazareth?" he had screamed. "Have you come to destroy us? I know who you are—the Holy One of God" (Mark 1:24).

"'Be quiet!' said Jesus sternly. 'Come out of him.' The evil spirit shook the man violently and came out of him with a shriek" (Mark 1:25, 26).

When worship ended, the news spread like wildfire. Everyone in town was talking about the events of the

183

morning. Fear of the authorities kept residents in their homes until after sundown. They learned, however, that Jesus had gone to Peter's home and had healed his mother-in-law.

As soon as the sun had dipped beyond the western horizon, "the whole town gathered at the door." There Jesus healed the sick, restored the cripples, and "also drove out many demons" (Mark 1:33, 34).

A short night

It was probably after midnight before Jesus was able to retire to the guest room at Peter's home. The next morning, when breakfast was ready, the Master had not yet appeared. The family and the other guests waited a bit. Then someone, probably Peter, gently knocked on the guest room door. No answer. A louder knock—but still no answer.

Finally, Peter pushed open the door. The room was empty. People started asking, "Where is He?"

"I think maybe I know," Peter said. "He has a spot out of town where He likes to go to pray."

Mark gives this simple report about what had happened:

> "Very early in the morning, while it was still
> dark, Jesus got up, left the house and went off to
> a solitary place, where he prayed" (Mark 1:35).

Breakfast is forgotten. Peter and a few others head out the door. The sun had risen about 5:00 that morning, with the first light visible around 3:30. Jesus, therefore, must have left the house about 3:00 a.m.

"Simon and his companions . . . found him" (Mark 1:36). In our imagination, let's join them as they climb up a hill to a clump of trees. They find the Saviour on His knees, with sunlight streaming through the branches onto His kneeling form. A look of peace is on His face as, looking heavenward, He finishes His prayer.

This is only one of some fifteen separate occasions of which the Gospels mention Jesus in prayer. We can truly say that He was a "mighty Petitioner" (See *In Heavenly Places*, p. 76).

Mighty in prayer

The adjective *mighty* doesn't refer to His mighty power, for He had laid that aside. "The Son can do nothing by himself," Jesus had said (John 5:19). Mighty describes, rather, His faith—the intensity of His concern, the depth of His feeling.

Of about fifteen mentions in the Gospels of Christ praying, Matthew mentions three, Mark and John each four, and Luke reports eleven of the fifteen. Compare that with the fact that in his Gospel, Luke focuses on the humanity of the Saviour. Luke wants us to see Jesus as someone very much like us—totally dependent on God for power.

Do you see what that means? We, too, can become mighty petitioners. We, too, have access to the same power that enabled Jesus to transform lives.

Earlier, we noted that "the eyes of the Lord run to and fro throughout the whole earth, to show his might in behalf of those whose heart is blameless toward him" (2 Chronicles 16:9, RSV). For "blameless hearts," the NIV says "fully committed" hearts. It's from this phrase that I drew the expression "fully committed disciples" that I used in Chapter 2.

Now let me paraphrase a little further: I believe the eyes of the Lord are running to and fro throughout Christendom and the entire world in search of fully committed disciples who will also become "mighty petitioners" as they reach out to seek the lost.

The first essential

I would like to suggest that to become mighty petitioners, we must first, like Apollos, become "mighty in the scriptures" (Acts 18:24, KJV). We need to become acquainted with the promises and commands in the Word—remembering that every promise and every command provide "subject matter for prayer."

Praying with an open Bible adds the power of the Word

to our prayers. Take, for example, the first promise in Scripture—the implied promise in Genesis 3:15 where God told Satan, "I will put enmity between you and the church." In that statement God is also saying to each of us, "I will help you to hate sin."

The unconverted heart does not naturally hate sin. That takes a supernatural work. And with our Bibles open to Genesis 3:15, we can ask God to give us that hatred. If we will then spend time studying the life of Jesus, beholding Him in this way will transform us (2 Corinthians 3:18). A hatred for sin—for anything that would hurt Jesus—will grow steadily stronger.

As we come to hate selfishness and pride and lust, we can then use Genesis 3:15 as we pray for others. In the might of that promise we can claim victory on behalf of those battling Satan.

The second essential

The second essential is to actually schedule time to pray. We probably won't need to get up at 3:00 a.m., as Jesus apparently did that Sunday in Capernaum. But we must do whatever it takes to have unrushed time for God's Word and for prayer.

Christ's preference for meditation and prayer seems to have been the early morning. So with David, who wrote, "In the morning my prayer comes before you" (Psalm 88:13). And again, "I pray to you, O Lord; you hear my voice in the morning; at sunrise I offer my prayer, and wait for your answer" (Psalm 5:2, 3, TEV).

Whatever the time or times you choose, you'll need a lot of "whatever it takes" determination until the habit is established. But stick with it. In his book *Yours for the Asking,* Edwin Gallagher says:

> "Having a regular early-in-the-day prayer time involves a lot of determination, planning, and self-discipline, especially at first. But you will be surprised at how quickly it can become a habit hard to break."[1]

A habit hard to break! That's good news!

Mighty arguments

As mighty petitioners, we can also use mighty arguments. To some it may seem irreverent, but the Bible contains examples of several of God's friends "arguing" with Him. Moses did in Exodus 32:7-14. After the Hebrew people had worshiped the golden calf, God tested Moses by offering to destroy them and raise up a new nation through his descendants (Exodus 32:9). Moses "argued" against this. The Egyptians, he said, would ridicule the name and works of God (Exodus 32:11, 12).

"Then," the record continued, "the Lord relented" (Exodus 32:14). Moses won the argument.

Nehemiah, as we saw in Chapter 2, used "holy arguments" as reasons why God should bless His people. Daniel does something similar as he confesses Judah's sins and pleads for Jerusalem. Note the two "arguments" in the following petition:

> "For your sake, O Lord, look with favor on your
> desolate sanctuary. Give ear, O God, and hear;
> open your eyes and see the desolation of the city
> that bears your Name. We do not make requests
> of you because we are righteous, but because of
> your great mercy. O Lord, listen! O Lord, forgive!
> O Lord, hear and act! For your sake, O my God,
> do not delay, because your city and your people
> bear your name" (Daniel 9:17-19).

Daniel's foremost "argument" is that Jerusalem and "your people bear your name." Because of that, He argues, You need to act for the sake of Your name. His second argument is "because of your great mercy."

As we pray for others, we can do so in the confidence that "nothing is impossible with God" (Luke 1:37). Proverbs 20:1 assures us that God can turn hearts the way nature sometimes turns rivers of water. As you pray for specific people, be encouraged by these words:

"We entreat the heralds of the gospel of Christ
never to become discouraged in the work, never
to consider the most hardened sinner beyond the
reach of the grace of God. . . . He who turns
hearts as rivers of water are turned can bring the
most selfish, sin-hardened soul to surrender to
Christ" (*Testimonies,* vol. 4, p. 537).

A lot to pray about

Denominational leaders estimate that on any given
Sabbath, more than fifty percent of the "on-the-books"
Seventh-day Adventist membership in North American is
not in church.

A recent report indicates that in my home state of
Michigan, with a membership of about 27,000, only
13,000 are in Sabbath School on any given Sabbath.

As we noted earlier, the August 17, 1992 issue of the
Pacific Union Recorder estimated that North American Seventh-day Adventist churches may have up to one million
missing young adults.

Such awful statistics call for fervent petitions and mighty
arguments on behalf of these missing members!

In my two churches, we have grown over the last thirty
months from 69 to 90 members on the books at Coloma,
and from 180 to 200 at Eau Claire. But a total of nearly 70
of these never attend.

A few have moved to other parts of the country and

I am spending an increasing amount of time praying
that God will do "whatever it takes" to bring non-attending members back to Himself and to the church.

haven't transferred their membership. Quite a number,
however, are local residents who currently attend no
church.

Occasionally I suggest to my elders—and sometimes from the pulpit, "Let's pray that God will do whatever it takes to bring non-attending members back to Himself and to the church."

"That kind of praying," I should always add, "needs to be accompanied with an outreach through personal contacts and friendship."

Names on three-by-five cards

During my 1992 mid-summer study break, I jotted the names of non-attending members onto three-by-five cards. I often carry these in my shirt pocket. I am spending an increasing amount of time praying that God will do whatever it takes to bring them back to Himself. As time permits, our elders and others are also making attempts to renew regular contacts with them.

We have already seen several stirrings in people's lives. Shortly after I began the above prayer lists, for example, my Coloma church received a note from a person who has not attended there for almost a decade and for whom we had no address. She now lives in another state, and included this note with a tithe money order: "Hope everyone is doing well. I think of you often. You probably don't remember me, but I surely have you on my mind a lot. Here is my tithe."

I have you on my mind a lot. Through our prayers, could this become true of tens of thousands of other non-attending members?

Generally I pray for those on my three-by-five cards as a group. One author suggests another technique that I am beginning to use: he intercedes for people and/or families one by one, by mentally going from house to house as he prays. To do this, of course, he must first visit in that home.

Billions of children and youth

"I invite everyone who is a Christian to please stand."

The request came from an evangelist as he spoke to a crowd of about 10,000. Around 6,000 stood.

"Now, if you became a Christian before your twelfth birthday, please be seated."

About half of the 6,000 sat down.

"If you became a Christian between twelve and fifteen, please be seated."

Half of those still standing sat down. By the time the speaker reached the fifties and sixties, only a handful of people still stood.

Statistics about the percentage of people who choose Christ before or during their teens vary. One publication has claimed that ninety-six percent of conversions take place in childhood.

And never have there been so many children! Statistics cited in Chapter 1 point to the fact that in many third-world countries, between forty and forty-five percent of the population is under fifteen. By A.D. 2000, one-third of the world's six billion people will be under fifteen years of age. At that time, the number of eight- and nine-year olds alone will about equal the population of the United States.

Jesus took a special interest in children. In Matthew 18:1-14, He talked about children and God's love for them. In Matthew 19:13-15, He blessed a group of children. In Matthew 21, a group of children crowded around Jesus after He drove out the money changers.

The Desire of Ages suggests that Jesus knew these children would listen to Him and accept Him as their Saviour far more readily than grown-ups (p. 515).

So also today. As a first step toward reaching more children in our neighborhoods, let's start praying for them.

As a beginning, consider arguments we can use in pleading with God on behalf of the two groups we have briefly mentioned: non-attending members, and the children and youth of our neighborhoods.

It goes without saying that these prayers should be followed by action—doing whatever it takes to contact these precious jewels.

Three "arguments"

Over this past year I have started using seven different arguments as I pray for my congregations, missing members, and new interests. Here are the first three:

1. The mighty argument of Calvary.

I see this as the most powerful of all arguments when we need to refute Satan's accusations against those for whom we are praying. It helps silence the accuser and gives God the right to work with additional power.

I first open my Bible to a crucifixion passage, such as those in Matthew 27 or John 19. Then I try to visualize the scene by asking, "What is there to see? What is there to hear? What is there to feel?" After a time of mediation, I may pray a simple prayer such as this:

"Father, your memories of Calvary are a hundred times more vivid than anything I could ever imagine. I see this scene as a mighty argument that gives You the right to act. In Luke 11:9 You have invited us to ask. I ask that You do whatever it takes to help this person feel a need. Do whatever it takes to bring him to the foot of the cross in repentance and faith."

2. Luke 15 and Christ's concern for the lost.

Luke 15 contains three parables: the lost sheep, the lost coin, and the lost son. In each case, a concerned individual—one with a "whatever it takes" spirit—sought that which had been lost. In every case, that which was lost mattered. And lost people matter so much to God that He was willing to do whatever it takes—even to sacrificing His Son—to save them.

With Luke 15, I like to combine the promises in Ezekiel 34 about the divine Shepherd seeking His sheep. God declares His intention to "search for the lost and bring back the strays"—to "bind up the injured and strengthen the weak" (Ezekiel 34:16).

When Luke 15 and Ezekiel 34 are combined with Calvary, we have another argument that silences Satan. It gives God the right to act in the full convicting power of the Holy Spirit.

3. Man's final destiny as pictured in Revelation 19-22.

Revelation 19 describes the return of Jesus as King of kings and Lord of lords. Revelation 20 tells about a thousand years of desolation on earth, the judgment of the lost, and the destruction of Satan and all his followers in the lake of fire. Revelation 21 and 22 tell about the New Jerusalem, the tree of life, and the river of life.

The central issue in these chapters is this: life and eternal joy, or regret and eternal death. No human being can grasp the magnitude of either.

Four more arguments

Consider four more powerful arguments:

4. The compassion of God as described in Psalm 103.

The psalm begins with praise, and I sometimes begin a prayer of intercession with the opening five verses of praise from this psalm.

I then ask God, because of His compassion, to give the blessings of those verses to individuals or groups. The fact that His compassion is like the compassion of a father for a child becomes a mighty argument for Him to act (Psalm 103:13). Almost every verse in the chapter can be turned into an argument for God to act.

5. The fact that where "sin abounded, grace did much more abound" (Romans 5:20, KJV).

Romans 5 is another chapter where you can draw from almost every verse as you intercede for others. I especially like to mention to God each of the five statements in Romans 5 that speak of His grace (verses 2, 15, 17, 20, and 21). Each is a powerful argument on behalf of those who are lost.

6. The fact that God "is able to do immeasurably more than we ask or imagine, according to the power that is at work within us" (Ephesians 3:20).

All of Ephesians 3 contains much subject matter for prayer when you pray for people. Verse 12 talks about approaching God "with freedom and confidence." Then verse 20 explains why: He is able.

Verse 20 also points to my responsibility: to live so close to Christ that His power will be at work "within" me.

7. The fact that God's promises are as certain as His "covenant with the day" and His "covenant with the night" (Jeremiah 33:20).

In an earlier chapter we noted that God mentions the above certainty three times in the four-chapter section of Jeremiah that is filled with promises of forgiveness and redemption (Jeremiah 31:35, 36; Jeremiah 33:20 and 33:25, 26).

Another faith-building discovery

In Chapter 16, I mentioned spending several weeks last summer in Jeremiah 30-33. I discovered that these four chapters contain more than two dozen gracious promises, and also some reproof. Within these are additional "arguments" for God to act.

This four-chapter section was given at a time when faith had hit rock bottom among the Hebrew people. Apostasy was widespread. Yet, in words of hope, these chapters look ahead to restoration and healing. Chapter 30, for example, includes these promises from God:

- "I am with you and will save you" (v. 11).

- "I will restore you to health and heal your wounds" (v. 17).

- "I will restore the fortunes of Jacob's tents and have compassion on his dwellings" (v. 18).

- "I will add to their numbers" (v. 19).

- "You will be my people, and I will be your God" (v. 22).

Chapter 31 is even richer, with promises that include: "I will put my law in their minds and write it on their hearts" (v. 33).

In chapter 32, Jeremiah begins a prayer with these words:

> "Ah, Sovereign Lord, you have made the heavens and the earth by your great power and outstretched arm. Nothing is too hard for you" (v.17).

Then, in chapter 33, God replies to Jeremiah, saying:

> "This is what the Lord says, he who made the earth, the Lord who formed it and established it—the Lord is his name: 'Call to me and I will answer you and tell you great and unsearchable things you do not know'" (Jeremiah 33:3).

"Call to Me." What a gracious and wonderful invitation!

"Turn the Bible into prayer," suggested Robert McCheyne, a nineteenth-century Scottish preacher.

If you are reading the first psalm, he suggested, you can open the Bible on a chair before you and kneel and pray. You can take the first verse, "Blessed is he who does not walk in the counsel of the wicked," and pray something like this: "O Lord, give me this blessedness. Help me not to walk in the ways of the ungodly."

You can go through the psalm and pray about each verse. "This is the best way of knowing the meaning of the Bible, and of learning to pray," he added.[2]

I do that in connection with my "whatever it takes" praying. A chapter at a time, I have "prayed through" Jeremiah 30-33. With every promise, I ask God to do "whatever it takes" to fulfill that promise for me personally—and for His people.

This morning, I used Psalm 100 as "subject matter for prayer." Then I wrote the five verses on a three-by-five card to keep with me so that I could use the ideas in later prayers during the day.

I included these prayer ideas as I talked with God while on a mid-morning errand. I again used Psalm 100 as prayer content while cleaning out a daffodil bed. (As I complete the final chapter of this book, it's still early February here in Michigan, but the first daffodils are already coming up!) An evening walk under the stars will provide another opportunity to pray through Psalm 100.

The content offers much "subject matter for prayer." It begins, "Shout for joy to the Lord, all the earth." The "all the earth" took my thoughts to other lands. Today is Friday, and as I talked to God early today, I figured it was about sunset in Siberia, so I prayed for Sabbath-keepers and all Christians in that land. Later in the morning, I prayed similar prayers for Europe.

Verse 2 encourages joyful songs; then verse 3 says, "Know that the Lord is God. It is he who made us, and we are his; we are his people, the sheep of his pasture." There's a lot to talk to God about in that verse!

"The Lord is good," the closing verse declares. "His faithfulness continues through all generations." As I thought about these wonderful truths, I asked God to do whatever it takes to awaken fervent gratitude in the hearts of His sons and daughters.

This repeated usage has helped me memorize the psalm. In the weeks ahead, I will probably use ideas from Psalm 100 many times as I converse with God.

Testing God

Give it a try! Pray through some of the shorter psalms, and through passages like Isaiah 53 and the Beatitudes. And converse with God also about some of the ideas in chapters like Romans 8, 1 Corinthians 13, Ephesians 2, Philippians 4, Hebrews 11, and Revelation 22.

Talk to God also about the content in Christ's prayer for unity in John 17. In Paul's time, the worst enemies of the unity of the church were within—the critics, the legalists, the fanatics. And speaking of her time, Ellen White wrote that one "indiscreet, high-tempered, stubborn-willed man" can do so much damage that "all the force of Seventh-day Adventists" would not be able to counteract his presumption and fanaticism (*The Ellen G. White 1888 Materials*, vol. 2, p. 482).

So today, the worst enemies of the Seventh-day Adventist Church are enemies within—the date setters, the critics of leadership, the fanatics. And because these enemies are *within* and because they seek followers, they often are able to destroy the unity Christ prayed for in John 17. Let's talk to God about that prayer with an unprecedented "whatever it takes" spirit!

One more thing!

The expression "whatever it takes" has almost unlimited potential. It can make your praying more effective. It can help deepen your commitment. And as you do your part in bringing about answers, it will strengthen your faith.

Through writing this book, it has become second nature for me to pray "whatever it takes" again and again during the day. It is my prayer that reading these chapters will help "whatever it takes" praying to become second nature to you also.

For me, a favorite activity is to mentally review the Lord's Prayer and then simply to pray, "Whatever it takes." If I could give a "homework" assignment, it would be to review the chapter in this book entitled "The Lord's Prayer and 'Whatever It Takes'," and then pray it on behalf of your own family, your local congregation, and the world church.

Let me close with these questions:

What might happen if, in their prayers, 10,000 believers would use the "arguments" suggested in this chapter—and others of their own drawn from Scripture—in fervent petitions to God? What if a "whatever it takes" commitment accompanied each petition?

Suppose, also, that it became a habit for tens of thousands of us to send dozens of "whatever it takes" petitions heavenward all through the day? Such a prayer is so simple that often you can pray it even while driving. What might happen if this became a habit with tens of thousands as we walked, drove, cleaned house, gardened, or whatever?

Would such petitions give God an opportunity to work with unprecedented power? Would it help us become fully committed disciples? Would it enable God to bring about the unity within the Seventh-day Adventist Church that is so needed today?

Prayer works! Let's test that assurance!

Notes

1. Edwin Gallagher, *Yours for the Asking* (Washington, D.C.: Review and Herald Publishing Association, 1978), p. 37.

2. Andrews A. Bonar, *Memoirs of McCheyne* (Chicago: Moody Press, 1948), pp. xix, xx. Used by permission.

A Dream

I believe that God has a dream—a dream drawn from the fact that His eyes are ranging throughout the earth, searching for people "whose hearts are fully committed to Him" (2 Chronicles 16:8).

As He dreams, God longs for tens of thousands of young people and believers of all ages who have fully committed hearts. He longs for them also to possess a "whatever it takes" spirit. He dreams, further, that these folk will be steadily growing toward unlimited confidence in Himself.

Fully committed hearts. A "whatever it takes" spirit. An unlimited confidence in God.

Then, in His dream, I think God sees these fully committed hearts coming to Him as mighty petitioners—men and women and youth and children who are developing what Paul calls "the mind of Christ" (Philippians 2:5). They are seeking to think as Jesus thinks, feel as He feels, hate what He hates, love as He loves, and pray as He prayed.

More! Much more!

As you seek that intimacy with God, what next? Here are four suggestions:

1. Do whatever it takes to assimilate more and still more of God's promises.

For nearly twenty years I have helped college students systematically underline eighty of the better-known Old Testament promises and eighty New Testament promises, along with forty command-promises. In the Appendix, I have listed 100 of these. Each provides what one author calls "subject matter for prayer."

You could first underline these promises in a distinctive color. (A blue grading pencil is excellent for Bible underlining.) Take one at a time, prayerfully consider it, and then talk to God about what it promises. Let faith in these promises strengthen you in every time of need and for every time of opportunity.

2. Secure some or all of the additional materials that have been prepared as part of the "Prayer Works!" and "Seeking His Spirit for Service" themes.

These include a book by Charles Bradford entitled *Find Out About Prayer*, a study guide by Kurt Johnson called *Prayer Works!*, video and study material by Ron Halverson titled *Prayer Warriors*, a prayer journal by Dwight Nelson entitled *A New Way to Pray*, and a *Holy Spirit Seminar* notebook by Gaylene and David Wolkwitz.

3. Make the Lord's Prayer a daily part of your devotional life.

Chapter 8 of this book summarizes the use of the Lord's Prayer as you intercede for others. For additional information about using the Lord's Prayer, I recommend the book I have cited several times—Pastor Bob Beltz' *Transforming Your Prayer Life*. He devotes a full chapter to each of its petitions. The format he suggests can help you develop devotional times in which you spend a half hour or even an hour in prayer.

4. Make listening to God just as important a part of your prayer time as speaking to God.

On this topic, the most helpful book I have found is Bill Hybels' *Too Busy Not to Pray*, which has a chapter entitled "The Importance of Listening." It's followed by these three chapters: "How to Hear God's Leadings," "What to Do With Leadings," and "Living in God's Presence."

Learning from Paul

Paul, like Christ, strongly believed in prayer. He sought prayer, first of all, for himself. "Finally, brothers," he wrote to the Thessalonians, "pray for us that the message of the Lord may spread rapidly and be honored, just as it was with you" (2 Thessalonians 3:1).

He also prayed earnestly for his converts. In Colossians 1:9-14, for example, he prayed that the Colossian believers might:

1. Be filled with a knowledge of God's will (v. 9).
2. Develop a heart that seeks to please God (v. 10).
3. Bear fruit "in every good work" (v. 10).
4. Grow in the knowledge of God (v. 10).
5. Seek the strength that comes from God (v. 11).
6. Develop great endurance and patience (v. 11).
7. Give thanks to the Father (v. 12).

As you seek to become a mighty petitioner, open your Bible to Colossians 1:9-14 and ask these blessings for yourself. Then make similar requests on behalf of those for whom you are praying.

You can be part of the answer to God's dream!

Life-changing Promises

Peter assures us that through Christ, God "has given us everything we need for life and godliness." The apostle then points us to God's "great and precious promises." Through these, he suggests, we may "participate in the divine nature and escape the corruption that is in the world caused by evil desires" (2 Peter 1:3, 4).

Listed here are forty Old Testament and forty New Testament promises—and twenty commands. The commands can also be appropriated as promises, for all that God asks us, He gladly helps us to do. Each is subject matter for prayer.

Here are three suggestions for making these promises a part of your devotional life:

1. Underline all promises in a distinctive color.

2. Leaf through these promises and review them a book at a time.

3. Open your Bible to a specific promise and talk to God about it. Include thanksgiving for what God is going to do as well as for what He has already done.

Old Testament promises

1. Genesis 3:15
2. Genesis 12:2
3. Exodus 4:12
4. Exodus 15:26
5. Exodus 33:14
6. Psalm 1:1-3
7. Psalm 34:7
8. Psalm 50:15
9. Psalm 55:22
10. Psalm 121:8
11. Psalm 126:6
12. Proverbs 3:5, 6
13. Proverbs 3:9, 10
14. Proverbs 4:18
15. Proverbs 22:6
16. Proverbs 28:13
17. Isaiah 1:18
18. Isaiah 26:3, 4
19. Isaiah 40:31
20. Isaiah 41:13
21. Isaiah 43:25
22. Isaiah 44:3
23. Isaiah 49:24, 25
24. Isaiah 53:5
25. Isaiah 54:17
26. Isaiah 55:6, 7
27. Isaiah 58:10, 11
28. Isaiah 58:13, 14
29. Jeremiah 17:7, 8
30. Jeremiah 29:13
31. Ezekiel 36:26, 27
32. Daniel 12:3
33. Hosea 6:3
34. Hosea 14:4-6
35. Joel 2:23
36. Joel 2:28-30

37. Zephaniah 3:17
38. Zechariah 10:1
39. Malachi 3:10, 11
40. Malachi 4:5, 6

New Testament Promises
1. Matthew 1:21
2. Matthew 6:33
3. Matthew 11:28-30
4. Matthew 28:18-20
5. Luke 1:37
6. Luke 6:38
7. Luke 11:9
8. Luke 11:13
9. John 4:13, 14
10. John 6:35
11. John 6:37
12. John 7:36, 37
13. John 8:31, 32, 36
14. John 10:10
15. John 14:1-3
16. John 14:13, 14
17. John 14:27
18. John 15:7, 8
19. John 16:7, 8
20. Romans 1:16, 17
21. Romans 8:28
22. 1 Corinthians 10:13
23. 2 Corinthians 5:21
24. 2 Corinthians 9:6-8
25. 2 Corinthians 12:9
26. Philippians 4:10
27. 1 Thessalonians 4:16-18
28. Hebrews 1:14
29. Hebrews 4:15, 16
30. Hebrews 7:25
31. James 1:5
32. James 1:12

33. James 5:16-18
34. 1 John 1:9
35. 1 John 2:1
36. 1 John 5:11, 12
37. Jude 24, 25
38. Revelation 2:7
39. Revelation 3:20, 21
40. Revelation 21:4

Command Promises

1. Matthhw 5:41
2. Matthew 5:44
3. Matthew 6:19-21
4. Matthew 26:41
5. Mark 6:31
6. Romans 6:13
7. 1 Corinthians 10:31
8. 2 Corinthians 6:14
9. Ephesians 4:32
10. Ephesians 6:18
11. Philippians 2:5
12. Philippians 2:14
13. Philippians 4:4
14. Philippians 4:6
15. Philippians 4:8
16. Colossians 3:2
17. 1 Thessalonians 5:16-18
18. 1 Peter 3:15
19. 1 John 2:15-17
20. Jude 20, 21